THIS TIME AROUND

MILESTONES

John T. Eber Sr.

MANAGING EDITOR

A publication of

Eber & Wein Publishing

Pennsylvania

Library of Congress
Cataloging in Publication Data

ISBN 978-1-60880-279-1

Proudly manufactured in the United States of America by

Eber & Wein Publishing

Pennsylvania

A Note from the Editor . . .

"In books I have traveled, not only to other worlds, but into my own."
 –Anna Quindlen, *How Reading Changed My Life*

Everyone who has ever had the privilege to possess a book has held a passport in his or her own hands, and everyone who has ever had the pleasure of reading has traveled more places than he or she could ever reach on foot as a consequence of deep meditation. Readers young and old rarely know exactly where a book will take them before cracking its spine, but they are usually confident embarking on a journey beginning in bound form will be significantly more affordable, convenient, relaxing and rewarding than many physical ventures. Voyages through verse in anthologies such as *This Time Around* are guaranteed to be substantially more varied than typical travel; and they are just as, if no more so, unearthing as many places our own two feet can take us. If a book is a passport, its content seemingly provides the evidential stamp of the reader's adventure. Be prepared: this collection of exquisite and extensive literary talent will take you to places you have never imagined, beyond the barriers of your personal experience and worldview to eclectic settings and situations you potentially have yet to even envisage. Deservingly, reading this array of dynamic poetics will also lead you deep into your own existence—allowing you to relate to other poets through the representations of human experience they have so carefully crafted, and causing you to reassess your own intuition, understanding and judgment of particular phenomenon of life through a newly heightened awareness of humanity.

As Anna Quindlen, American author, journalist, and Pulitzer Prize-winning opinion columnist for the *New York Times* notes, books take us "not only to other worlds, but also into [our] own" in ways only aesthetic experience affords. Because reading causes us to examine ourselves—our pasts, presents and futures, our loves, losses and limitations and our overall human condition—collections of poetry prove invaluable. Sadly, our busy lives often prevent us from seriously considering *ourselves*: our personal histories and how our living biographies are continually shaped by whatever we have done or whatever has been done unto us, whatever we are currently in the act of doing and whatever we hope or fear to engender in days to come. Furthermore, a disappointing handful of people are mindful enough of how social consciousness necessarily cultivates knowledge of self. Admirably and gratefully, poets are some of the chosen few who essentially realize this; even more impressively, poets propagate greater appreciation of this awareness through the dissemination of their individual accounts in poetry.

Thankfully, one of literature's innate advantages is found on each page of every book, in the way each page commands a reader to pause and perceive what he or she has just read. The kind of self-reflection fostered by literature is priceless, because it takes us to a place of understanding and—willingly, eventually—peace. Hopefully, this compilation will excite your own reflections. While thoughtfully consuming all the provoking poetic narratives collected within these pages, make sure to ask yourself: Where will your reading take you *this time around?*

Rachel Rogers
Editor

The Dragonfly

While trekking the woods one day,
I noticed along my way, a beautiful sight, I'd say.
The flicking among the flowers,
Diving and weaving with colorful showers,
In and out and down the spout, flying in and flying out—
And many more joining for a vast array of summertime
beauty:
An awing array.

Alice Browning Randell
Sunrise, FL

Autumn Leaves

The leaves have all turned red and gold
Most all the trees are stripped bare
Few leaves still cling to their lofty perch
They cling with the gentlest of care
They know when it's their time to fall
To fall from their lofty perch
Whether from elm, peach or lofty birch they fall
Float to Earth with the greatest of ease
And they're forever to be
Watching the snow as it's falling
And landing on old, Mother Tree

Ronald Thaler
Wheat Ridge, CO

Sharing and Caring for All

In life do you ever catch yourself complaining about the load you've been given?
How about you take a moment to stop and think of all you have and thank the Lord that you are just livin'
And how about all those that live in a country and have far less than we do?
What about all of those people that have died in war-struck countries, think now that could have been me and you
Maybe if we all started to think of others instead of ourselves and think of others that have far less things and wealth
and those that have little or no medical supplies to assist in providing good health
Imagine if we all started caring and sharing, maybe we could start a worldwide trend
With just simple acts of sharing and caring we could watch this old world start to mend
Caring and sharing deserves to be handed down and remembered for all to know
Here is a saying that goes like this:"It's not what you take when you leave this world,
It's what you leave when you go!"

Gary Hall
Rock Falls, IL

Diversity

It's all about you and me,

the secondary differences between us and our primary
similarities.

Talents, ambition, and abilities
make it easy to see the uniqueness of our diversity.
Learning to know rather than assume, knowing one day our
tolerance will improve. The benefits outweigh the
negativity when we naturally accept people for their
diversity.

Engage yourself thoughtfully, when learning new cultures
try to avoid the terms *his* and *hers.* Be color blind to quality
and more accepting of not just one, but *all* for their
diversity.

Take pride in what you know and not just what you see.
And remember it's all about valuing you and me when it
comes to. . .*diversity.*

Nichelle Montano
Auburn, CA

*I had my children at a young age and it caused me to work very hard to
accomplish short and long term goals. I have learned a lot about tolerance
and valuing diversity having grown up poor and with a career at a large
corporation for the last fifteen years. I have been certified to deliver diversity
training to staff in an effort to bring awareness that we all play a roll in this
awesome world and if we accept each other for our uniqueness, we will
live more fulfilling lives. Peace is key; remember it's all about you and me.*

The Mother's Psalm

The Lord is my copilot. I shall not rush.

He maketh me to hit all the green traffic lights.

He leadeth me through shopping hassles.

He restoreth my composure.

He giveth me strength to make ends meet for
my family's sake.

Yea, though I walk through the valley of laundry,
I will fear no evil, for thou are with me.

Thy perspective and sense of humor,
they comfort me.

Thou preparest a table before me with the
assistance of take-out.

Surely clutter and confusion shall follow me
most of the days of my life, but I shall dwell
in a happy home forever.

Amen

Kelby Ochoa
Vail, AZ

My Wishes

The evening sky darkens, the stars will shine bright,
But which is the first star that I'll see tonight?
I wish that I may, oh, I wish that I might
Have everything that I wish for tonight

I wish to have an outfit for every day of the year
Why, that would be dear
Not a smudge, not a smear
How fun it would be to get one every year

I wish every hot day the schools
Would be cool
No one would sweat like a mule
Or look like a fool

I wish no one would hurt others
Not fathers, not mothers
Nor an annoying brother
No one would hurt others

And then in the morning, I'll wake with the sun,
My dream won't be over, my dream's just begun
A dream full of goodness and laughter and fun
For me, for the world, and for everyone

Brooke Fairchild
Warren, NJ

The Circle of Friendship

The circle of friendship is a place of warmth and caring
We friends come together for listening and sharing
A place of kindness and trust—of tears and laughter
I'm glad to share that circle with a special friend like you

Marjorie A. White
Urbandale, IA

Beast

There's a beast, a monster,
And it has me by the throat
It's getting harder to breathe
The more I struggle the more it hurts
Its talons are digging deep. . .
Dragging me down
Down
Into the abyss
There is no escape
I can't run from myself
The monster is me
And there is nothing I can do

Cora Garrison
Calgary, AB

Blocked

Trapped in an enclosed space, and it's locked.
Escaping isn't an option,
because my mind thinks of plans that my body can't perform
and

I have ideas that no one seemed to previously understand,
so
I stay here, waiting for an opportunity to fly into my hands.

Opportunity.
It comes at you like gargantuan waves in the sea,
but some people miss it. They focus on things that should be subsequent
to *intelligence* and follow independent views so
they remain stagnant, their lives full of recurring hues.

Time,
Is what I have on my hands,
when what I need is that opportunity. But instead, I'm here
recalling the instances which life had already presented.
Not all were great, but at only seven and ten, those instances seem
as if they were just a *midsummer night's dream*.

Dream.
Many occur like threads unraveling from a tight-knit seam,
Revealing things that the conscious mind chooses to ignore,
so
we pleasure ourselves with thoughts of our "innocent" fantasies,
and reality sets in; it sets sail on the waves of that gargantuan sea.

Talaisha Midy
Winston-Salem, NC

Hidden Treasure

There is something about a lovely sunny meadow
That does not need a tree.
It lies there laughing, shouting,
Come!
Come play with me.
The sun and rain caress me.
Wild flowers
Steal colors from the rainbow
To dress me.
Come!
Share my glee
And seek my hidden treasure!
Raise your eyes straight overhead.
Can you see, can't you see?
Straight up there is eternity!

Virginia E. Gardner
Albuquerque, NM

Mr. Spider

All night a web you spun,
In time to catch the morning sun;
Now loaded with a late night dew,
The world wonders, how you do.

Decorated with a million jewels,
A place the fly and you will hold duels.
You created a lot of beauty before sunrise,
Mr. Spider, is this something you realize?

Diamonds and rubies reflecting
As you sit silent waiting—expecting
The fly or hornet or the wasp
That will soon give their last gasp.

Your jeweled threads are not all beauty,
Not to the unfortunate visiting bee.
I wonder, was it a good morning to die
Under the gentle blue sky?

Edward Finn Jr.
Fort Atkinson, WI

Forgive Me for Leaving

When we were together
We had hopes and dreams forever.

Then the days came one by one
And all at once I knew the time
had come.

I watched you cry that last night
And I have had many dreams of
that night.

We grew so close those last few days,
I didn't realize how much I loved
and cared for your ways.

And now I'll be coming home and I'll
never let you part,
because now I know you mean
something special deep down inside
my heart.

You see of all these words I could
not find the three simple words
That will always make you mine:
                              I love you.

Ronald O. Hill
Ogdensburg, NJ

Dabble

I've dabbled in this and I've dabbled in that,
to learn about this and learn about that,
but now I'll take on a new journey you'll see—
how to put on a page things about you and things about me.
I'll dig and I'll pry way down in my mind
to bring up some memories of where I was blind.
I'll jot them here and I'll jot them there,
about crazy things that just jump up and stare.
So with paper and pen I will carefully write,
sometimes in the morning and sometimes at night,
but however I dabble, I know it will be,
some awesome poems about you and about me.

George Farnsworth
Gold Beach, OR

To Fill My Bucket

I am eighty years old now—and I just cannot believe it,
All those moments and acts abide with me, bit by bit
But oh, so many things I never took my time to get
During these final acts, I will think how to fill my pit!

Well, I never saw real Irish green or any travel limit,
Now I could read great writings by that English Brit,
And see old artists' masterpieces I've missed, I admit,
But I'll revisit so many old friends and places—and sit!

God—we've spent so many joyful memories of benefit,
May I keep on remembering them until I have to end it?

Etta Mae Preston Alexander
Rochester, MN

I was born on December 5, 1932 in a small railroad town in Hume, Illinois—a population of a hundred twenty-five people then—two hundred nineteen now! I was the third girl and fourth child to Mima and William Joseph Preston who left their family and friends after marriage in Naugatuck, West Virginia. I attended kindergarten, PS No. 31, Butlet University and lastly Indiana Central College until I met my husband there, John Alexander from Rochester, MD. He graduated—he was two years ahead of me. We got married in September, 1953. I worked at Santa Monica College in the personnel office and attended classes there. Finally, I went to Loyola University and got my BA in English literature from the new LMU (Loyola-Marymount University). Then, my second son was born in Santa Monica and I went to Santa Monica-Malibu Unified School District where I stayed for twenty-five years and loved my work there! My husband, John, passed away in 2004, so my boys and I moved to Rochester, MN, where there are so many relatives we can't keep track of everyone! I'm enjoying my retirement and catching up on my reading and writing.

Unbound

Lay flat
Face down
Motionless for forty years

Hating all movement
Hating all sound
Hating himself

But always planning, replanning self-murder

Sits up now
Startled
Looks around
Stands, walks, looks for the trash to take out
Looks for something to go get from the store
Something to repair
Something to paint
Someone to talk to

Someone to be

Then stopping
Remembering . . .
Remembering that far person in that other world
The one before this started
The one before he was bound

The one for whom smiling faces held open all the doors
and he strode through them
as would a prince

Michael Joseph Penner
Lawrence, KS

Blind and Blinder

There was a man named Carver
Who at one time
Was blind all the time
He just didn't know it

Then he met a man named Robert
Who was naturally blind
Robert was blind all the time
And he sure knew it

Carver and Robert met one night
And it seemed like they knew each other through life
Over Scotch on the rocks and a couple of hooters,
Carver got blind and Robert got blinder

Both men learned about each other
and the night became morning
Robert preferred color TV
Carver wanted to go bowling

For both men it came to a drawing
Although they could drink in church
A piece of paper and a pen
Brought two men together
Friends to the end

Wayne Hovden
Porterville, CA

Marriage

Marriage is an institution
Marriage is a bond between two
people
Marriage should be held in high
regard and respected
Marriage should be cherished
Marriage should be between a
man and woman like the Bible
states
Marriage can be hard
and very rewarding all at
the same time
Marriage should last forever
if possible
Marriage is a love that a man
and woman have that can stand
the test of time

Christina O'Connor
Omaha, NE

A Family's Like a Tree

A family's like a tree—
always related to me.
Growing, growing, limb by limb,
breathin' life, oxygen.

A family's like a tree—
providing protection, weathering the storm—
offering healing, mending from a prickly thorn.

A family's like a tree—
providing food, shade, standing firm,
strong roots from which to learn.

A tree is like a family—
offering shelter if need be . . .
a family's like a tree.

Lori Garcia
Houston, TX

With Gratitude to Millie the Dog

So tiny and loving, in need of a home,
she melted our hearts like nothing we'd known.
Her eyes hopeful, sweet, and full of trust
she had to be ours, to be always with us.
As soon as I saw her, a name came to me;
she would be "Millie," that was plain as could be.
She jumped, she played, with her ball she ran;
at first sight of our baby . . a loyal fan.
Late one night when the baby cried,
Millie wanted to go outside.
She ran out on the deck and only God knows
why this innocent creature was injured so.
Lying on the vet's table, her eyes filled with tears,
she kissed the baby to help calm her fears.
Her legs didn't work, but hope and love were there.
Then months of treatments, medicine and sweet loving care . . .
along with tears and lots of prayer.
First, a small tail wag then a miraculous step,
a lesson in attitude and faith when its kept.
Now it has been nearly thirteen years,
we have celebrated Millie with joy and tears.
She is a stoic lady and demands much with no words;
we are grateful each day that our prayers were heard.
We love our little Millie dog, now frail and hair of gray,
the gifts that she's brought to our hearts and our home make us grateful
every day.

Julie DeRose
Williamston, MI

My husband, daughter, and dogs, Millie and Tinkerbell, live on a small lake in Michigan. After a severe back injury, the miracle of Millie's recovery through the power of positive attitude, determination, love, and faith is what inspired me to write this poem. My family's journey with Millie the past twelve years has inspired our lives. I hoped by writing this poem that the reader would feel the love and hope and be inspired in some way, too.

Tomorrow

Tomorrow I hope to see you, it has been too long that much is true
Some things are out of my control
If I had it my way, son, my mind and body would be whole
I have to work with what God gave me and pray that He will save me
Your mother, she loves you but may not know what is best for me or you
If I could I'd be there, son, when the morning has begun to see the first light of
Dawn touch your face, make you breakfast, wipe your face
One day I hope you'll understand I care and never had the upper hand
I love reading to you when we are together, it makes me wish the moment could
Last Forever

Nathan Dickson
Safety Harbor, FL

One with Earth

People say I can light up a room with a smile
I say the smile in me is light for thy. He says
my tears fall as rain, I ponder the thought—no
shame, I say I'm one with earth for all it's worth.

They question my mood, Mother Earth,
don't know what I'm feeling or one's worth.
I say I'm one with Mother Earth for all's worth.
My presence is calm, cool and collective as can be—
a sunny day, light clouds and a bit breezy, that's me!

My flip mold side effects can wreck havoc
for all it's worth so please be gentle and kind
to Mother Earth. With all the mass destruction,
criminal abduction and unequal injustice no wonder
the world is flushing. Katrina, Sandy, Irene, and
Tornadoes mean twister disaster and tsunami screams.

Running from terror in our area, family strides and
dried on the waste side. Now do you see why?
Mother Katrina, Sandy, Irene, tsunami and
tornado—homi was so lethal due to our own evils
not treating one as an equal.

I say I'm one with Mother Earth, for all it's worth, please
be kind and gentle to all here on Earth.

Sorry to all families, for all it's worth, please forgive Mother Earth.

Tisha Stewart
Wilmington, DE

*I have two sons, Stewart is three and Kingston is eighteen months. Life,
nature, people, places, and things inspire me. I'm a true believer in a higher
power and believe all things are possible. I've always considered myself a
writer, actor, doctor, lawyer, producer, editor, reporter and so forth. I'm
now stepping out there. People take life for granted, that's what inspired this
poem, "One with Earth."*

The Wait

I anticipate your arrival,
I go through the motions
of getting ready,
pretending to be occupied
with nothing.
A quarter past each hour
I make excuses for you
not materializing.
The phone rings,
I answer cheerily,
talking to the no one at home.
As the receiver is fondled,
you fade into a voice for my roommate.
And it's yet one hour, not too late
so I sit down and work on your coming.
At the next ring,
I pass up an opportunity
to make a new friend the following night.

Sherri Levin
Beverly Hills, CA

My first book of poetry sits nestled in a drawer under copies of tax returns. Inside the covers of the black and white composition notebook, the words of unrequited love rhyme with hope and sparkle in perfect fourteen-year-old cursive. The red journal sits on my desk. In it, the handwritten prose of early adulthood. My musings needed an audience. That audience was pen and paper. I went to sleep for a time. I woke needing to catch up to my past, to reignite what was never extinguished. My new journal is blue.

Unbreakable

I'm the one
I'm the unbreakable
It's building inside me
I want to fight back
My pride is stronger
My self-worth is more

I'm the one
I'm the unbreakable
I must listen to my head
Remember who I am
As life tries to cut me down to size
There's no chance

I'm the one
I'm the unbreakable
With feeling loss of control
As the walls of doubt grow higher
Still my spirit is not broken

I'm the one
I'm the unbreakable

Renee Herman
Windsor, CT

Part of my inspiration for this poem is that I am a traumatic brain-injury survivor. With the love and support of my family, they have showed me how to live each day to its fullest: to be unbreakable with the good, the bad, and the indifferent. Believing in yourself can be one of the hardest but most rewarding jobs there is. Poetry is my way out, a healthy way to live an uncertain life. One full of more questions than answers, yet more possibilities than one can count.

Arrival

Feed me—feed me—feed me
The rain dispersed all night
Droplets still negotiating their complete downfall
Noting spring's arrival
The flowers were screaming with thirst
Feed me—feed me—feed me
I need to grow from the earth
To feel the luxury of living
Sprouting amazing hues of colors
Never a duplicate grows
Feed me—feed me—feed me
Perfuming the world with their individual fragrance
I want to live and feel the sun in the morning
With the early dew which helps me grow
After the darkness escapes away
Feed me—feed me—feed me
It's my moment in life
I am here
Dressed magnificently
For my arrival
Feed me—feed me—feed me

Renata Dawidowicz
Madison Heights, MI

Listening to Country Music

Listen to the music
Let the country songs relax and groove you
Let the rhythm and melody move you
Feel it in your soul and heart

Listen carefully to country music
You will understand the message in the lyrics
It's where you want to be

Turn up the volume
Get lost in the music, you're in the zone
Keep it country, I like it that way

Living every single moment
The life and the dream

Turn up the radio
It's the kind of song to sing and dance to
When it comes to country music

The music you want to listen to
Don't go without
Let the song move you
Feel the melody and rhythm
Be proud, blessed and grateful you have country music

Danielle Elizabeth Barry
Myerstown, PA

Danielle Elizabeth, twenty-three, is a Virgo and a native of Schaefferstown, PA. She has been writing poetry since she was twelve. The purpose of writing is to express herself. Danielle has been listening to country music all her life. She is encouraged and inspired by country songs and she loves it. This poem is dedicated to country music fans and country singers. In addition to writing, Danielle's interests include photography (a butterfly photo is in a 2013 calendar), playing guitar, gardening, collecting seashells, reading, dancing, horseback riding, Mother Nature, animals, talent shows or solo dancing, and fashion shows.

God's Gift

A babe in swaddling clothes
    Came on a dark and silent night
Without music, without trumpets,
    To bring us God's own light.

He brought our Lord's soft touch of love
    To reach the hearts of all,
That we would know compassion
    And forgiveness when we fall.

Thus this wish travels far and wide
    Going from heart to heart
That we may know God's always there
    Even when we're apart.

A blessed Christmas now is wished
    For family and friends most dear
That will carry the joy of Jesus' birth
    Into every day of the year.

Charlotte Bertram Potter
Marion, WI

Since 1962, I have been writing my own original poetry plus other poetry for special occasions. As a retired math teacher and minister, I have been blessed to have my poetry read at many churches.

Edwin Tyler

Ed was an angel sent by God to love and care for me,
But with all of my tears and all of my fears, I could hardly see
Oh, what more could I ask for, what more would I need,
Than an angel from Heaven to come and rescue me?

I can see him playing his fiddle, I can see him teaching school,
I can see him in his garden, going hunting and fishing, too.
These were his hobbies, things he really loved to do,
But my angel from Heaven left me too soon.

I was working and praying God would help me survive,
But I didn't know he had an angel come to live by my side.
Ed loved me and he helped me until death did we part,
My sweet angel from Heaven left me with a broken heart.

Ed's waiting now in Heaven for me to get there,
And it won't be very long til Heaven's glories we'll share.
We'll sing and play forever around the heavenly throne,
There'll be joy and happiness such as we've never known.

It has been four years and we still all miss you,
But you are always on my mind.

Lucille Tyler
Liberty, TX

The Worst Day of My Life

The day my mom cried and my dad walked away
She wasn't herself in her own way
I tried to feel her pain

The days went by; the tears, they dried
But there was always pain in our hearts
The day my mom cried and my dad walked away

She worked all the time with pain in her eyes
When she came home all you could see were tears in her eyes
I tried to feel her pain

Joy came back and always a little hope
But it didn't go that way
The day my mom cried and my dad walked away

She was filled with joy and love
And help from above
I tried to feel her pain

I know through all of this there were rough times
But I knew things would be fine
The day my mom cried and my dad walked away
I tried to feel her pain

Lisa Regimbal
Yabima, WA

Soul-Tie Blues

Soul-tie, soul-tie, release me,
For I've been exposed to darkness.
Heal every piece of my fragmented heart.
Restore my trust and set my soul free.

The first time I saw him, I fell in love—
Dressed in seductive black, dark eyes flashing,
Tall and becoming, the silver-haired fox.
Request answered, sent from somewhere above.

Strangely familiar, like someone I knew,
As if we'd been together before in the past.
We promised each other to ride the waves
—As long as the excitement lasts.

We began as acquaintances and bent all the rules.
Moved from friends to lovers; forged the unholy tie.
Lies and betrayal soon took their toll,
Living the double life, playing the game of fools.

Hidden bondage revealed, love turned to hate,
We reached the point of no return.
Reality has spoken, it's not meant to be.
Bonded by tragedy, separated by fate.

Soul-tie, soul-tie, release me,
For I've been exposed to darkness.
Heal every piece of my fragmented heart.
Restore my trust and set my soul free.

Dianne Kaye
Roseburg, OR

*I'm a retired counselor and family therapist and encountered many courageous
clients during twenty years of human services work. Their stories are my
inspiration. I've been blessed with mentors who took me under their wings,
three marriages and three wonderful sons. I've loved and been loved, buried
a husband, father, son, brother, and mother and watched a lifetime of friends
pass through. The poem, "Soul-Tie Blues," depicts the story line of a fictional
piece I'm writing: a romance-suspense novel about the trials of a woman who
travels to Dusseldorf, Germany to recover her family fortune. Watch for it!*

The Beauty of a Woman!

The beauty of a woman isn't
in the clothes she wears or the
expensive jewelry she wears but in
her smile!

The beauty of a woman isn't
in the way you make her feel but
deep in her soul!

The beauty of a woman isn't in the
luxuries you can buy her but what
you do for her when it comes from
your heart!

The beauty of a woman can't be found
like a summary of a book cover but
it lies deep within her heart!

The beauty of a woman gets better
and better the older she gets because
it's not the makeup she puts
on every day to feel good about
herself but when you simply tell
her she's beautiful when she's all
natural and laying around in
her pajamas!

The beauty of a woman isn't about
what's on the outside but most
importantly, it's in the air she breathes
and the blood that runs through
her veins every day and night!

Misty Arnold
Odessa, TX

Respite

As my tense, dry body slipped softly below the hot, oily water's surface,
I gently pressed the stiff, but pliable, plugs into my ears.
My hearing faded away—so slowly,
So silky—like a pat of butter melting in a hot pan.

I thought I could hear the soft sizzle of bubbles.
I thought I could hear my pulse.
I was caught up in a transformation. From barking dogs, blaring TV,
fussy baby to—
Nothing.
For a moment, I thought I understood Emily Dickinson. Obsessed with
the theme of Death, she revered its peace.

A half-hour was but a second.
I arose from my fountain, my body warm and dripping.
My finger resisted reaching for my ears.
I re-entered those bars of fabric.
Oh, those stupid dogs.
Oh, this is a good movie.
Oh sweet daughter of mine, I missed you while I was away.

Renee C. Ballenger
Cedar City, VT

Life

I've learned so very much
But I'm sorry to say
I didn't practice much of it
As I traveled along life's highway

For if I had I'd surely know
For me and my family
The mountains that I had to climb
Would not have been so hilly

So let this be a lesson
To all that's starting out
Don't let yourself be deceived
That you know what life's about.

Joesph Milton Adams
Waxahachie, TX

I have no formal training as a poet. My father was an avid writer of poetry; he also had no formal training as a poet. I inherited my love for writing from him. My father wrote poems on paper sacks or anything that was available when he got the desire to write. He wrote a memorable poem the night he sat up all night with my sister who had pneumonia at the time.

The Passing Years

The years are passing much too fast
I cannot bear the strain
Desperate, I reach to hold them back
But, oh, it's so vain
It hurts, it hurts to see them go
And drain my life away
To see strong hearts grow very weak
That once were young and gay
I can't, you can't, do anything
To slow them down at all
I must, you must, face up to it
Age makes the strong ones fall

The months, they pass so swiftly too
I cannot believe my eyes
Think of those years, where have they gone?
It's hard to realize
When as a child to see one old
Would hurt me deep inside
Now look at me and you will see
The wrinkles I cannot hide
Where can I run? Where can I hide?
There is nothing I can do
Why should I buy? I cannot own
For I'm just passing through

Emmett E. Capes
Rochelle, IL

Mother June Lillie

The time is never right for the loved ones left behind
Your daughter's here
I'm with you as I write these words, under a tree,
a nice warm breeze, just you and me surrounded with flowers.

I feel so overwhelmed. How do you write for the one you love and
gave you life?
I promised you I wouldn't cry because you told me to stop, so I reached
for a Kleenex and found Dale's handkerchief, the one he said to keep.

My love is never-ending and each day I cherish our love even more.

Be at peace and sleep softly as I whisper in your ear, "Your daughter's
here," and you reply, "And so is sweet Jesus."

As we tightly hold our hands together, I remember all the times you held
my little hand and took such great care of me.

As you drift so gently away, I say, "Your daughter's here, and I love you
very much
for all the times that you know so very well, just you and me."

As we look at each other, our eyes hold the special bond between us
which will live on within our hearts always.

Mother, as you told me, "Look up in the clouds above. I will be
tucked away when I'm called home, sweet sugar, for I shall always be
with you,
your mother's here and we are in the Lord's hands."

Jeanne C. Obrenovich
Nokomis, FL

*I was born in Norwalk, OH, graduated from Milan and finished my college
education with a master's from BGSU. Growing up on a farm, my parents
taught me to care for animals, work for goals, enjoy nature, and the simple
things of life. Working my way through college I met my lifetime mentor and
friend whom I helped establish a lifetime endowment through BGSU (Dr.
Joseph F. Krauter). I wrote the poem straight from my heart for a beautiful
mother so fitting for her. My mother sacrificed with a smile, loved, and valued
her children first!*

The Lake

Tonight
Although Swan Lake's matinee came
From a mythical place,
It has returned to us
And the planet
As the feminine
Changing face

Before
I witness ballerinas
Mimicking swans
Spread all over the stage
Strewing off feathers
To first take a stance
On the bank
Reflected as womankind

As dancers not as a sisterhood
They tumbled and tussled each other
in the throes of their technique
To reach the realm
Of *prima artiste*

Until the second act
Rushed in the human prince to
Reconcile the rivalry
By choosing the Swan Queen
as his wifely bride
To finalize the ballet's last act
As a marriage ceremony
After which the new woman,
Resident in her rank,
Introduced a larger audience
To the lake

Eleanor Rosman
Yonkers, NY

Awakenings

As I kneel down by the hospital bed,
I lower the rail and touch her head
Her snow-white hair and translucent skin
Reveal her age, and the time she's been an angel on earth

Her eyes are open: they're pale and blue,
She's looking at something distant and true
A subtle smile, a peaceful look, a vacant stare,
It makes me wonder, "Are you there?"

Let me hold your hand so you will know
That you are loved and we all care
Let us guide you on your way,
Until we meet again someday

As I look up from my hospital bed,
A hand reaches down to touch my head
A face so kind and caring is looking at me. . .
No, she's staring

Is that a tear in your eye? Please don't cry
I've had a wonderful life here on earth,
Now it's time to move on
To life's final stage after birth

I'm trying to speak, but the words won't form. . .
Please understand, my hands are cold, but my heart is warm
From inside this body, my soul reaches out—
My heavenly Father is calling me now

Thanks for holding my hand and trying to understand. . .
Thanks for your care and your tears,
And most of all, thank you so much for holding me, dear
Goodbye, for now. . .

Lydia Ray
Fairfield, PA

Life's Path

One being can change the world.
You're put on this earth for a reason;
Whether you realize or not, there's a higher being
With a deeper meaning.
Keep on dreaming.
You'll find your way
One day.
Admit it or not, you have a lot to say.
Outgoing or shy,
Give it more than one try.
Allow your voice to be heard, you may just make a difference.
Express yourself,
Have a little faith—
You won't succeed if you sit around and wait.
To God I pray
I will be happy for all of my days.
You have to get up and try;
Before you know it, it will be your time to die.
Fulfill your destiny because it is set in stone
By God alone.
The choices you make will lead you in the right direction;
God has you under his protection.
Be true to yourself,
Be true to God.
Let go, let God—
And life won't ever seem that hard.

Alyssa Mazzoli
Staten Island, NY

The Art of Love

A good marriage must be created.
In marriage, the little things are the big things.
It is never being too old to hold hands.
It is remembering to say, "I love you," at least once
each and every day, it is never going to sleep angry,
it is having each other's back, it is having a natural
sense of values and common objectives, it is standing
together facing the world, it is having the capacity to
forgive and forget, it is the search for the person you
needed all your life and it is the young and the
beautiful, the restless, the sexy, the hot, the angel,
the devil, but most of all, it is the feeling of love at
first sight, knowing that you can't live without
the other person.

Laura Nowell
Brockton, MA

The Rainbow

There are rainbows for everyone to see, but ours has
been special—meant for you and me—with all the colors
ever so bright—strong enough to light up the night—to
lead us the way—along to our journey's end—we have
pursued our dreams each day—the good and the bad we
encountered along the way—as we get close to the
rainbow's end we reflect on our life together—sadly though
we're together we must reflect it alone—your thoughts are
hidden in your mind alone—but you give a smile that
says it all—to let me know—you know me as I know
you—we will meet over the rainbow—rest in peace

Joseph L. Daigle
Lynn, MA

*"The Rainbow" was written by me as a memorial for my wife, Catherine
C. Daigle, on May 5, 2013.*

Haunted

I feel you in my sleep
and I know it's not a dream,
'cause what I feel
I feel so deep.
But when I wake, you are not there,
you are gone, you've been gone for a year.
Sometimes I hear you whisper to me
loving words you hope will heal me.
But, as long as your presence is here,
I remain haunted year after year.
I know you mean well,
you're just trying to break me out of my shell,
but I can't move on unless you do.
So with these last words I say,
I love you.

Kristie Fox
Sedalia, MO

Dark Room

I was living in darkness, a very dark room
I lived in destruction, the darkness of doom
A light begin to shine high in my face
I didn't know the light was God's loving grace

I followed the light from this dark, dark room
Leaving destruction and ready to bloom
I fell on my knees and I heard a voice
Fear was within me, I had no other choice

The voice said, "I have a plan for you"
I fell on my face, I didn't know what to do
I was there for a moment or even an hour
The light was so brilliant, high in power

I was faint and frail, I knew nothing at all
I was afraid to stand, I thought I would fall
There is no darkness, there is no gloom
Jesus drew me out of the dark, dark room

Georgie Hughes
CRP Christi, TX

Christmas

Christmas was nearing and seen everywhere,
Store wrappings and Christmas lists discarded there

From the presents we all brought and the fun we all had,
We will always remember and always be glad

The charge cards had flourished, the people were merry,
They bought everything that their arms could carry

And hurrying home in great secrecy,
Wrapped all of their gifts for under the tree

The big morning came with the breaking of dawn,
The gifts were distributed, each one had gone

To a beaming young face or to someone called "Hunny,
The paper, it flew, we sure looked funny

The smell of roast turkey hung in the air,
And odors of minced meat made with great care

'Twas time to get rid of our diets and such,
Just sit down and ate til we ate too much

Next year at Christmas, God willing I know,
We'll all be together as a Christmas ago

Helen Gilmore
Kitchener, ON

Song of Siomha

From the midst of Scathach Forest comes a howling piercing wail.
Its sorrow burrows in so deep a gentle skin so as to weep.
Past flowers underneath protective leaves of green, a woman peers into a
wood transformed by mystic means.
Whispering leaves caress her skin and curious, she is lured within.
Her feet move silently ahead, purposefully and without dread.
Translucent, her white nightgown glows and through the trees with
ease it flows.

The wailing stops.

Deafening is the silence as it lingers in the air.
An illusion seems the woman's frame, like a ghost without a name.
An eerie stench of sickening death rolls in a fog with its hot breath.
Wicked trees break through the earth and taunt the air with hateful mirth.
Their twisting fingers touch the sky on gnarled arms from trunks held high.
Vines snake along the ground and curse the earth without a sound.

Sharp claws fly from a wall of blackness.

From the midst of Scathach Forest comes the woman's piercing wail.
Her sorrow burrows in so deep a gentle skin so as to weep.
It is too late to turn around for thick vines wrestle her to the ground.
She beats at thorns that claw her flesh and rip her gown into a mesh.
An angry hiss flies by her ears and soon the darkness disappears.
Soft leaves and dirt create a berth and she is swallowed by the earth.

Amanda Kroll
Elgin, IL

Purely Purified Purity

Skies dazzling like emeralds
Clouds exploding with color
My ears caressed with the song of the heralds
Filling my lungs with purity and power
Eyes closed toward the coming storm
Life's beauty so pure and yet so average
When the rain falls I shall not be forlorn
I shall embrace it untamed and savage
And crying tears over discovered harmony
I leave this place behind
Pushing on toward the golden sea
Though I shall miss the purified grind
Of the herald's tune within my ears
Presenting me with hopes and dreams
Chasing away all of the deepest fears
Oh, how wonderful were these things
My own bright and hysterical laughter
I will not remember after
While I continue to avoid all possible logic
Hand me another shot of the sweet tonic

Daniel J. Payne
Bel Air, MD

My Guardian Angels

From darkness to light
My life is a journey of pure confusion
Total chaos
Traveling ever toward the light
Sometimes stumbling back
Knowing always the goal in mind
Is pure light and pure consciousness at the end
Sometimes I feel the struggle is not worth the pain
I have lost so many loved ones
The pain is so sharp
Every day living with a knife being twisted in my heart
But not moving forward means I am falling back
All the people that I have lost and now
I am trying to lead the way
My tribute to them, my hope for myself
Is to keep moving forward
To keep pressing on
I can feel their strength even though they are gone
From the sight of their favorite flower
The smell of their perfume
The smell of old cigars
Suntan lotion and catching fireflies late in the afternoon
When I am falling back
It is what keeps me pushing on

Amanda Moyer
Homer City, PA

Hare Hollow

In the small peaceful village
there is an enchanting store,
you gasp with delight at the beauty
as you enter the front door.
Beguiling teddy bears greet you
wearing sweaters of red and blue
as playful bunny rabbits
flirt from the shelves with you.
The lovely candles flicker,
leaving silhouettes here and there
with heavenly scents of fruits and spice
wafting through the air.
Sweet music floats softly
giving a sense of calm
or a happy feeling just to sing along.
At Christmas time the place is all aglow
with Santas and snowmen
and trees covered with snow.
Like an enchanted cottage—
when one enters, others will follow—
a delightful, exciting visit
to the shop called—
Hare Hollow

Betty L. Mills
Granville, OH

Who Cares?

A man stands on a hill
In the dead of night the air is still
A shot rings out that shatters the sound
With a hole in his head he falls to the ground
But who cares?
Not the man who shot him, he's too busy fighting a war
Nor his wife and family, the news has not yet reached their door
Two boys fighting on a hill, a crowd gathers yelling, "Kill, boy, kill"
One boy flashes a knife
And with one angry slash, takes his foe's life
But who cares?
Not the crowd on the hill
They're just looking for a cheap thrill
Nor the boy, he's too busy running in shame
Trying to make some money and hide from whence he came
A man says, "The war is over today,"
But revenge goes on from day to day
If not by gun or sword
It is passed on by mind and word
The son of the man that died on the hill
Swears, "I must get revenge, I, too, will kill"
The father of the child who lost his life
Cries out for revenge with his heartbroken wife
So who cares?
I have searched the world over
The only answer I would like to find
To the one question that plagues my mind:
Who cares? Can you tell me who cares?

Michael W. Scott
Hamilton, ON

I was born in Toronto, ON, Canada in 1958. I have experienced a lot of tragedies in my life that were difficult to rise above; as a result, I gave up caring as I felt that nobody else cared. Today, life is much different. I'm a college graduate and I share my life with my wife and son and I try to help those less fortunate. I have always enjoyed writing and have written other poems as well as a book that I hope to have published someday.

Springtime in Seattle

Soft gray clouds floating o'er my head
Like a warm downy comforter covers my bed.

Bare trees, the color of leather,
Left wet and naked by the winter weather

Sprout icicles, green and fat,
Hanging down from maple leaves,
Springtime hats.

Rhododendrons—red, violet and blue—
Awake from gardens in every hue.

Ah! The daffodils, see them toil
Poking up through sleepy soil.

It's springtime! It's springtime! At last! At last!
It flies to summer, so fast, so fast.

Gretchen Kaman-Fisher
Tacoma, WA

Dream

A restless mind too tired to sleep
Laid out on a bed of rock where moss and mice and other small things
share comfort
The sky
Blanketing a slumber that never comes
On a dark quilt that floats above, he reads the stars that spell her name
They trail through a valley yonder near hills and toward a luminescent
glow
On tired legs he stumbles
Weary of his travels he waltzes through city streets
Her face reflects on every window
Her hair billows off every head faced away
Her voice sings through every sound
Etched into his heart by beams of light that pierce the sky through tiny
pinholes
His restless mind tires of an endless search
He pulls the blanket down from the ceiling of the world and the stars
twirl about his body
Swirling from his toes and spiraling to his head
She swims between him and his blanket
She paints his lips with her kiss
It washes over him like a tide that drags them out to sea and together
they feed the sky to the ocean
As the stars drink their skin and spill them out into the universe
Sketched in space
They are the stars that illuminate the rocks where moss grows and mice
sleep
And their blanket, the sky, nests upon their dreams

Kevin Cumming
Toronto, ON

Dedicated to my love, Jessica Ylanko.

A Tribute to My Husband

Did you ever truly realize all the lives you've touched,
Or the impact that you had on those you loved so much.
Your sweet and gentle nature put everyone at ease,
You always did what was needed, you did everything to please.
But then things changed, the cancer came, and life turned upside down,
The alternative route is what we chose—to California we were bound.
We really could not comprehend what the doctors had to say,
But your positive attitude to beat this beast grew stronger every day.
Yet the miracle that we prayed for was just not meant to be,
Though you tried so hard to fight the fight, too soon you had to leave.
Every day without you now since you had to go,
Is like summer without sunshine and Christmas without snow.
Those last days were so difficult, our emotions running high,
I'm thankful for those final moments we all got to say goodbye.
My once-happy heart is hurting, so much pain and sadness there,
And tears fall from my eyes, when I see your empty chair.
I wish that I could talk to you, or have one of your "Herb Hugs,"
Could you send one to my broken heart from your new home up above?
I'll always feel you close to me and though you're far from sight,
I'll search for you among the stars that shine so bright at night.
And if you're looking down on me and you see me laugh or smile,
Just don't assume that I'm okay, 'cause I'm missing you all the while.
I know they say life must go on, but it feels like it's all uphill,
My heart still hurts, it hasn't healed—I'm not sure it ever will.
I love you to the moon and back. . forever.

Robin Mitschele
Hawley, PA

A Child Was Blessed

A child was blessed
If only for a moment
The love of her daddy
Given the gift of believing
That heaven is never too far
They say it takes a minute
To find a special person
An hour to appreciate them
A day to love them
An entire life to forget them

David R. Wayne
Kellogg, MN

I have two sons. I'm over seventy years old and have four grandchildren. I have two great-grandchildren. I like to tell stories to the kids. I take care of my mother, she is in her nineties. I like to play cards and I'm working on a book.

No More in Vain

No more a monster
Behind the door
No more a slave or servant
To world's misery
No more to be a lame mind
That goes nowhere
Thank you, Jesus
Thank you, Lord
For bringing me through
An open door of no more
A life lived in vain
But a betterment to me
And in the world I want to be
No more living in yesterday
No more in vain
I learned much but found
I left a lame mind
Henceforth bring me new
To serve God and country
A betterment not in vain
A freedom I wish
Made new from old
Assure this day, thank you

Betty Shriver
Mogadore, OH

A Prayer for All Seasons

Lord, I need some explaining
Please don't think that I'm complaining
But lately I sort of feel surpassed.
My family is all healthy and though we're anything but wealthy
We are happy and that's all that one can ask.
Were it not for education I wouldn't have this situation
I wouldn't have the ability to read
About athletes and the owners and their monumental boners
As to salaries, free agency, and greed.
It seems once these men were humble and like all of us they'd fumble
But were happy for the opportunity to play.
So they worked real hard at playing and their mothers kept on praying
And it wasn't long till they were on their way—
To the higher scales of wages and although it came in stages
It exceeded anything I ever had.
I was always told that COLA
And a five percent should hold 'ya
Plus the fringes—I should be awfully glad.
So I'd take them up on their offers
I put money in the coffer and help out so the kids could graduate.
Now for three more years 'twas most like
There'd be no further pay hike and I never thought to re-negotiate.
Now, something sounds real funny
The athletes say it's not the money
It's the principle, or some hogwash like that.
But they also have a mentor
A money hungry "ten percenter"
So they ask for more regardless of their stats.
I know that I sound cynical but being analytical
A homonym comes evident right here.
Take the too-much-used word *principle* and substitute *principal*
And lo, the proper answer will appear.
I'm sure I must sound jealous and perhaps I'm overzealous
But there's one thing I wish that they would heed:
When they stand up and holler for the almighty dollar
It's not principle, it's unmitigated *greed*!

Dean Ormsby
Livonia, MI

I Think of You

I think of you often and wonder how it would be,
If you hadn't married her, but instead, me.
I see us happy day after day,
Letting even the bad times not get in our way,
Of becoming as one in spirit, flesh, and mind,
With soft words of love expressed and never unkind.
To focus on making each other complete,
With a touch, a kiss, an embrace, and gaze so sweet.
And through the years we walk in love as husband and wife,
Telling each other sweetly that you will always be the love of my life.
I think of you often and wonder how it would be,
If you hadn't married her, but instead. . me.

Rebekah Arvin
Indianapolis, IN

*I am a watercolor artist, wife, mom, grandmother, baby boomer, Hoosier
born Filipino/American. I love music, art, and all things related to beauty. My
poem was inspired by "what if" (I hadn't married my husband of forty plus
years), the movie* The Notebook, *and the challenge of writing a meaningful
message in rhyme about love.*

Number Seventy-Three

Seventy-two years have come and gone.
So many times I have gone wrong.
Now looking back I mostly see
The joy, happiness, and God's gifts to me.
The heartaches and sickness only made me strong.
It helped me to be an arm to lean on.

I did my best to raise three—
God's precious gifts He gave to me.
My true mate was hard to find.
I kept looking and God again made the right time.

My prayer for now is to remain strong,
Not be a burden to anyone,
To meet my Lord while in my garden
With all His wonderful gifts from
The ground, would yet make my
Short life the best all around.

Dina Howard
Abindon, VA

Ode to Aging

As a young man in my prime,
A stronger body you could not find.
My bulging muscles I could flare
And throw my body in the air.
I'd twist and turn—jump and bend,
On exercise I could depend
To keep my body in a mend.
But time has taken its heavy toll
Upon my body and my soul.
For when I try to perform
The leaps and jumps that once were norm
This aching body tells me true,
This is not what I now can do.
Where rippling muscles used to be,
Just sagging skin is all you see.
Don't feel bad, I have been told,
That's how it is when you grow old.

Jesse P. Jones
Cudahy, WI

Dear Society,

I'm tired of your judging,
can't we just stop
with all the pushing and shoving?
Listen, you've gone too far.

Does my forwardness alarm you?
Or are you afraid of the things I'll get to?
Like how you love to think
there can only be perfection in everything.

Or how you enjoy making people feel bad
because they have that touch of extra fat.
'Cause you think nobody's good without a thigh-gap.
How about you stop with all of that?

Don't you know,
not everybody can afford Forever 21 clothes?
And so what's in fake nails and snapbacks?
Girl please, I'd rather get my money back.

Society, you no longer rule me
because I woke up and saw how it's supposed to be.
I'm disappointed that no one has gone so far,
they finally got to see how beautiful they truly are.

And so many of you don't realize how great you could be,
if you would set yourself free
from these unspoken rules
of society.

Jenae Liaiga
American Canyon, CA

Minutes

Every minute of your life spent
Worrying about what other people think,
What they say and do,
About the future, the past—
Things you know you cannot change—
These are minutes that are stolen from you.
A minute may not seem like much,
So stop and think a minute.
They make up hours, days, weeks, years—
Eventually a lifetime.
So respect your minutes for they are a gift.
Each of us are given only so many.
They are a privilege so many take advantage of.
So take a few of your minutes every day,
Think about what's really important
And live your life that way,
Because you never really know
when your minutes will be taken away.

David Hobbs
Salem, AR

*I'm fifty years old and a born again Christian and recovering alcoholic, addict.
I believe God, faith, and doing the next right thing is the only way to fight
addiction. I was born in a small town in central Illinois. I now live in a small
town in Arkansas where I'm happily married and we manage a small car
lot. Cars and music have always been my passions. I've always liked writing
poems and song lyrics but this poem has always stood out to me. I wrote it
in a couple of minutes in a rehab center and believe it was a message to me
as much as anything. I've always wanted to share it because that was one of
my problems, worrying what people thought. I now believe in making the
most of every day, laughing often, helping others, and love.*

In Land of Ice and Snow

In the land where all the angels come by car, by bus, by foot
Where mentors guard their every move to spare them from the boot. . .
The test is more than some can bear, but easy for the others
And minds that wane will wane no more from harassment of their
brothers
The weary and the fit unite in Spartan face-to-face
And every day we make it through with stamina and grace
This is the land of snow and ice where we must watch our druthers
Lest any of our peers run back to tell the holy mothers!
Digging through the snow is only half the battle
Slipping on the daunting ice is sure to make nerves rattle
Bolts are not for horsing around, only good behavior
But our little angels can't compete in the everyday endeavor
They toil at tasks, that most repel, with nary a thanks or notice
And keep to themselves like the lily pad that balances the beautiful lotus
Our time in here is nearly done; we gave it a good go
And we'll be back tomorrow, in the land of ice and snow

Lynda Powers
Belvidere, IL

A Ring and a Kiss

The birds and flowers remind me of you
when the sun is bright with its warmth and glory.
The trees are green and the sky is blue—
it reminds me of a beautiful love story.
A story of two becoming one
spiritual strength with Jesus in our midst.
The beauty of a life which has just begun,
inspired by love with a ring and a kiss.

John D. Poore
Springville, IN

Winter Is. . .

Seeing people going ice skating
Going outside and seeing the snow fall from the sky
The smell of cookies in the oven
The apple-smell from the candle
The taste of cherry pie
The taste of the cold snow
Hearing people singing
Hearing kids playing in the snow
Feeling the cold snow going down your shirt
Feeling the cold ground after you jump a ramp
Winter is wonderful!

Greg Serena
McMurray, PA

I Am Keeping It Real

If I keep it parallel that means I am keeping it straight
And if I am hard to love that means I am easy to hate.
    If I ever turn fragile that means I am easy to break,
So I am going to keep it concrete and step out on faith.
    When it comes to change, I usually put up a fuss;
When in order to prosper, I must adapt and adjust.
    Losing is not an option—I have too much ambition
I can't stop—I won't stop, as I continue my mission.
    I am the fly on the wall—I look and I listen
And I stay on top of my game, so that no one catches me slipping.
    Momma was the Energizer, the Duracell is Daddy and
When the two got together, I was born forever ready.
    I am not saying I am the best, I just believe in what I do,
And I am going to stay on my feet like the soles in my shoe.

E. LaSean B.
Ragland, AL

The Internut

Of all the strangest friends I've ever met
One had a weird obsession with the Internet.
Instead of enjoying his deserved retirement
He doted on information electronically sent.
Why didn't he think of the Rocket and other fine cars?
And pause to remember the college days' bars.
Recall the time spent with Walter P. and the Deuce
And what about Bob, Candy, Fred, and the Moose?
No, it's software, monitors, bytes and other stuff
Give him modems, Microsoft and no useless light fluff.
Pentium, CD-ROM drive, mini tower and Windows 95
Let him get to the keyboard so he can really thrive.
For him it's the Net, the *netty, netty net netcha*
He's going crazy staring at that blank screen, I betcha.
Someday, maybe something will appear and he's out of his rut
And my strange friend will no longer be *The Internut.*

Fred Yahrling
Westminster, CO

Henry Starr

I've been to places far and wide,
    in all I've had to run and hide
I became very strong and wise
    And learned to go through town disguised
I had the fastest hand in the West
    yet many tried to challenge the best
And ended up with a bullet in their chest
    The government tried to give me
a bad name
    but really I've won this game
For I died of old age not
the gun of a man laughing
in my grave
    My body given back to the land

Esela A. Arzate
Brownfield, TX

Oh, How I Love Thee

Oh, how I love thee,
You sweet ephemeral rose.
A perfect being one day,
One devoid of the usual ethereality the next.
Here I am in Elysium
And you're bleeding on the floor.
I'm covered in your blood,
The euphoric torpor is setting in.
You struggle to breathe as I hold your heart;
Your own blood chokes you.
I drop to my knees and clasp my hands,
Lean close to hear your death rattle.
"Why?" you ask and I whisper back,
"Because I love you, m'dear."

Now I awaken in a drunken haze,
The crust of your crimson life-water a thin patina on my skin.
My eyes, my eyes! I can't believe them. They lie so cruelly to me.
All I see is your mangled corpse and I cry.
I dazedly totter over to you and drop to my knees, a cruel genuflection.
Hand in yours, the razor slices the skin.
Skin rends, crimson flows, darkness comes.
Together, even in death, I'm coming, my *amor*!

Adrian M. Haut
Momence, IL

The Sands of Time

The sands of time are calling
sweet memories are here
I walked a road of promise
I erred and played the fool

The sands of time are calling
sweet memories are here
Her charms were not forgotten
She was my everything

There was time
Time for friends and lovers
When love was my crown of glory
The thrill of my dreams
Made up for sighs and tears
But now the sands of time are calling

I think of the good times
I think of all she meant to me
I think of all the good times
Think of all it might have been

Think of all it might have been

Jorge Guevara
San Diego, CA

I Had a Little Girl

I had a little girl—cute, of course
Problem is—she thought she was a horse

She always wore boots as she cantered around
Stomping and pawing as she thundered the ground

Blonde curls bouncing as she trotted by
Give her room or she'll kick you in the thigh!

I noticed it early—with no remorse
Her first word spoken—and she said horse!

I thought she'd talk early—but I was wrong
She whinnied and snorted as if a sweet song

She's grown up now, but nothing did change
Still talking to horses like home on the range!

She rides 'em and trains 'em, and sells them afar
She'll take a horse any day—over a car

Her smile is contagious—her laughter outrageous
Her mark on the horse world loving down through the ages

Then one day—a knock on the door
'Twas a handsome dark-haired man (o'-war)

He came to see her stallions this day
She was wearing boots and shorts and riding a bay

She told her mama it was love at first sight
He loved horses like her—so it must be right!

Jackie Tone Polk
Stockton, CA

Summer

Horses in the field eating fresh green grass
Winter is gone, the cold air has passed
The sun in, out once again
The creek is flowing with newborn fins
Animals are out of hibernation
School is out for summer vacation
Summer is here, let's scream for joy
Summer is here, oh boy! Oh boy!

Judyth Caroline Patterson
Rutherfordton, NC

The White Frog

Back in the Ozarks there lived a rough and tumble character that went
by the name Ciric Renyenelds. Spring was coming and Ciric was about
bursting to play a prank or two. He would do anything at the drop of a
hat just for fun.

There were white spots floating over a meadow as one passer-by
described it, and then for a while there was nothing more heard
about white spots until some years later. It was reported that they had
a side show that involved white rabbits. Thanks to one of the circus
people talking to the manager of the town, they figured out that Ciric
Renyenelds was playing tricks again with his painted white frogs.

Kathy G. Kennedy
Jamestown, TN

The Old Sycamore

My sister, Bar, was almost three
When we played
Under that massive tree.

The huge, thick branches
Covered the ground—
With beautiful shade,
We could run around.

The long rope swing,
With a wooden seat,
Let us leisurely swing
Without touching our feet.

Often our bare feet
Would touch the grass
Until the path they made
Would forever last.

Way up to the sky
And then back, and low,
We'd sing in the breeze
And at times, drag our toes.

Those summers were fun
And our lives, carefree.
We'll never forget
Our sycamore tree!

Virginia D. Wells
Danbury, CT

Farm Living

Ten little siblings,
Growing up on a farm.
Early in the morning,
It was off to the barn.

Cows to milk—
Twice a day.
Fields are ready,
To bale the hay

Had to plow and plant,
And harvest the crops.
A big garden to weed—
The work never stops!

Didn't make much money,
But they were healthy and able,
And raised all the food,
That was put on the table.

Living on the farm,
With big open spaces,
Builds confidence and character,
You can see in their faces.

Farming is their living,
They are proud of what they do.
When the harvest time is over,
That means food for me and you.

Margaret Alexander
Smyrna, DE

I was raised on a farm outside the small town of Kenton, DE. I presently live on one acre of this farm. I am one of ten children. There are three brothers and six sisters. Living on a farm taught us the importance of working together and, yes, even when we didn't want to! I enjoy writing poems. My poems are based on actual facts and events that have taken place in people's lives. Poems are my way of expressing the things we take for granted in life, experiences that help shape our lives and character.

Us

We started our life without any clues,
It was you and me and those shoes.

We have fumbled and tumbled our way through this life.
You as my husband, me as your wife.

With our homes and our hurts we've had many a foe.
All odds were against us, as we both know.

I have seen us build and build some more,
Building and building the walls ever more.

We each have hidden behind our walls,
Each afraid of our possible falls.

We each have had our frights and fears.
We have fought them it seems with blood, and sweat, and tears.

We have handled them differently as some will cite.
You with your hiding, me with my fight.

As we face this latest foe,
It's more than a picture as you well know.

This foe has no name, but she has a face.
At times she wears nothing, at times it's lace.

Why, why, why? Why is it this way?
I need answers to these questions, I say.

I cannot find the answers for you.
With probing and searching, that's for you to do.

Janice M. West
Findlay, OH

Our Nation's Cry

Dear heavenly Father
We look to You up above
To give us Your guidance
And show us Your love

The terrorists came
Though we don't understand
Why they hijacked our planes
Tried to destroy our precious land

Two beautiful towers
Now lay scattered
Suffering is tremendous
Lives are all shattered

Numerous lives have been taken
Husbands, wives, many a friend
Not sure why it started
How and when it will end

Our nation is weeping
Our grieving is real
Please be with us
And help us to heal

We're asking You, Jesus
We're down on our knees
Send us Your angels
Keep us safe, dear Lord, please

Heidi Hayes
Broken Bow, OK

Heart of Anguish

standing
for more
than
just
a cause
when
those flaws
lead to
sunlight
with a
passion
to
fight
preferring
to capture
this dream
of
poetry
forever
these words
are
molded
to be
a
part of
me

Joe Smith
Markham, ON

6-12-05

I wasn't much for history.
But there's a date that will live in me.
It's bigger than any president's address.
It's bigger than landing on the moon I guess.
6-12-05 was the day I came alive.
6-12-05 was like a roller coaster ride.
It may not mean much to someone like you.
But it was the day all my dreams came true.
I prayed and prayed this moment would come.
I thank God each day that you're the one.
If I had to be with someone else,
It just wouldn't be the same.
I'd take you over having fortune and fame.
6-12-05 is more than an anniversary.
It was the day I met you and you met me.
I fell for other girls a lot of times before.
But you gave me so much and a whole lot more.
If I was to do it with someone else.
I couldn't go on.
The ways I feel for you,
They can't be wrong.
6-12-05 will be the day that lives in me forever.
Because that was the day for us to be together.

Michael J. Adamchick
Forty Fort, PA

I live in a small town in Northeastern Pennsylvania called Forty Fort. I am forty years old. I have no wife or kids, but I do have a mother named Alice and a brother named Paul; my father Daniel is deceased. I wrote the poem "6-12-05" as a testimonial to a relationship I had with a girl back in 2005. I thought she was the one but somehow she got away. Oh well, maybe the next one will be the one for me. But until then I'll keep on waiting.

Sin

Not just skin deep, it reaches even to the heart
Hate to love and love to hate, Jesus set my soul apart

Not just pleasure, it deals even to my pain
Live to die and die to live, Jesus take it away

Not just blindness, it covers even the voice
Pray to hope and hope to pray, Lord make Your way my choice

Not just the weak, it fights even with the strong
Win to lose and lose to win, Jesus make it gone

Not just the lost, it walks even with the found
Hide to run and run to hide, Jesus stand my ground

Not just at first, it comes even to the end
Ask to have and have to ask, Jesus forgive my sin

Stephanie Williams
Casper, WY

"If we say that we have no sin, we deceive ourselves and the truth is not in us. If we confess our sins, He is faithful and just to forgive us our sins and to cleans us from all unrighteousness," I John 1:8-9. "Blessed is he whose transgression is forgiven, whose sin is covered," Psalm 32:1.

The Therapeutic Touch

Therapeutic hands can lightly touch
But they never say a word
Even though they make no sounds
They tell the therapist so much
What area hurts and why it does
How to work with the area and make it better
When you lie down and relax
All your cares go away
Such a comforting gift
To have such knowing hands
To be able to help pain go away
Being able to release wayward thoughts
And bring us peace of mind
Healing hands help me so much
There's never a need to ever fuss
When you awaken and it is still the same day

Sharron Dorst
Janesville, WI

Bawdy Mary

Mary Jo ran a house, a most bawdy scene
Her girls were ladies, if you know what I mean
Night after night I would watch the parade
The varied arrivals, a curious charade

Old Mary would yell a welcome hello
And into the house all the men would go
Skinny ones, fat ones, men of all kinds
To the house they would go for pleasure to find

I'd see old Mary at places in town
She always smiled and never would frown
A happier person I have never seen
She was a curiosity to a boy of thirteen

The night burst with a piercing scream
Exit a man with a face wrinkled, mean
Slowly I saw her blood-stained breast
Three days later they laid Mary to rest

They shut down the house and barred up the doors
I waited and waited but men came no more
Mary was buried away from the town
A simple stone marked her spot in the ground

The funeral was hurried, not many were there
I wondered why so few would care
It was rainy that day, a cold lonely scene
A preacher, a grave, and a boy of thirteen

William Harper
Carlsbad, CA

*I have always loved poetry. I particularly love words that rhyme. My favorite
poetry has a distinctive rhythm that flows smoothly throughout that poem.
"Bawdy Mary" is one of my earliest poems and tries to capture rhythm
and flow.*

Camouflage

I am the pearly-white smile, peppered hair and designer suit.
I am a speaker. It hides the fact that I'm a cheater.
I want all the loot.
I am the college loan.
I am the studio apartment you call your home.
I am the one that you will pay back or I'll take everything you own.
I am the cheap food you consume in your
little room.
I am the cancer that follows, and
the healthcare you will need while in despair.
I am the prisoner.
I am the one you offer your life to.
I am the one who tells you to fight when
I ignite feuds.
I decide who you see on your television.
I decide which people on your television receive criticism.
I am the prescription pill commercial.
I am the list of symptoms.
I am the addiction. I am not a healer.
I am that song all over the radio, the one about
the wealthy drug dealer.
I will never reveal the obvious. I am out to steal your consciousness.
I am not the solution.
I am what the problem is.

Micheal Gamarano
Glendale, AZ

Grandma's Little Girl

Grandma, I was thinking of you today and a smile tickled my face
Remembering all the things you taught me, like always to say grace.
I remember sitting in your lap as you read a book out loud;
To hear me sing a song made you proud.
I remember those days laughing as I watched you fix your hair;
I remember crossing the road and hear you scream, "Girl, you stop right
there!"
I remember the goodness you put in me,
Though I know sometimes it doesn't show.
You played a special part in my life, and I thought that you should
know. . .
My life is filled with memories of you that I couldn't buy with all the
gold in the world
And even though I'm growing up, in my heart I will always be
Grandma's little girl!

Brooke Powell
Covington, GA

A Light Exists in Spring

A light exists in spring,
Not present in the year
At any other period,
When March is scarcely here.

A color stands abroad
On solitary hills
That science cannot overtake
But human nature feels.

It waits upon the lawn,
It shows the farthest tree.
Upon the furthest slope we know
It almost speaks to me.

Then as horizons step
Or moors report away
Without the formula of sound
It passes, we stay.

A quality of loss
Affecting our content,
As if we had suddenly encroached
Upon a sacrament.

Wendy W. De Guise
Oronoco, MN

Eye of the Needle

The eye of the needle, a rich man's despair
      His treasures are gathered on Earth with no care
God's golden gates stand open wide
      But worldly riches have no place inside
The eye of the needle, a rich man's distress
      The love of money is hard to repress
Diamonds and rubies are many men's dream
      Drawing desire with their glitter and gleam
The eye of the needle, a rich man's unrest
      The search for salvation an unending quest
Temptation and greed will trouble man's mind
      For wealth and power are ties that bind

The eye of the needle, a poor man's relief
      The "path to paradise" is to simply believe
Blest is the house that serves the Lord
      A home in Heaven their righteous reward
The eye of the needle, a poor man's release
      His faith in God will bring him peace
Debt and doubt will worry the soul
      But wise is the heart with "glory" its goal
The eye of the needle, a poor man's respite
      Sins are surrendered, burdens made light
The road to Heaven is trodden with care
      On bended knee, in solemn prayer

Tracey L. Vandekerkhove
Milkeytown, IL

I have been married to my husband, Mike, for twenty-eight years. We have two sons—Ty is twenty-five and Treg is twenty-three—and a daughter, Remy, is twenty-one. I attend the Greenwood United Methodist Church, a small country church with a warm congregation. God is my inspiration, my church family is my encouragement, and a close, loving family is my support. My thesaurus is my constant companion.

The Garden

The garden is so pretty I hardly can explain
The garden is so pretty though it needs a drop of rain
The cat stretches across the bench
Oh, look! I see a baby finch

The birds come to have a drink
While the crickets sing, sing, sing
The flowers are in bloom
Oh, rain come soon!

The butterflies fly across the sky
With the clouds passing by
The trees in the garden are growing up to the sky
With each inch of the garden there is adventure inside

Kasey Cochran
Avinger, TX

Missing My David

When will all this crying stop,
how can I make a deal
do I stay in bed and sleep all day
so I just won't have to feel?

In sleep I know that I can dream
and pretend that you're still here.
Awake, all of my heartfelt grief
knows nothing we now share.

You can't come over every night
with Angel and a pup.
Never again will I hear you say,
"Hey Mom, we're here. Wassup?"

I miss those times together,
not seeing you every day.
My family is much smaller now,
another son taken away.

Maybe God needed my David
in his heavenly family up there—
another angel to light the way,
another memory to share.

We all must leave this Earth some day,
our bodies and souls will depart.
Until my time comes—your memory
will stay within my heart.

Willetta Pat Steiner
Lebanon Junction, KY

The Vibrantly Beautiful Flower

She was as a vibrantly beautiful flower

The only one of its kind

But slowly she began to wilt
    and fade with time

Each year her vibrant colors
    seem to slowly fade

And her body seemed to bend
    and be swayed

Until there was left only a
    withered and dying flower

Bent from the years as slowly
    they bypassed

And swayed by the storms
    of life

But leaving behind a memory of beauty that
    is in all its glory—truly unsurpassed!

Vibrantly with colors she did bloom

And those who once looked upon her beauty
    can still see her

Tho' now she's slowly fading away

Never more to bloom upon the Earth

But to go to a better place to bloom
    eternally day by day

Once again as a *vibrantly beautiful flower*

The only one of its kind—

Maggie R. Thompson
Crowley, TX

Lullaby for the Next Seven Generations

If I could leave you tall trees
thick woods and fertile soil,
if I could bequeath to you
eagles soaring in crystal skies,
if I would endow you with
fresh flowing streams
and oceans clear and clean,
and fish and fowl and beasts
intact and thriving
on an earth unmarred by
vestiges of man's indifference,
if I would change a fright-filled world
power-mad and greedy—
then I must pledge to you my time,
and wealth and strength.
Far better this
than toys and games
and knitted things
and jars of homemade cookies.

Althea Ockerman
Brighton, MI

Woe Is Me!

Where is the inspiration?
If only I could find pearls instead of coal,
I could reduce my desperation!

Where is the word, or thought, or emotion
to express more clearly the need for serenity
in the midst of all this commotion?

My thesaurus slowly gathers dust
while appointments eat up time and energy.
Projects and wishes sit anxiously on the shelf.
How do I adjust?

Ronald Downey
Prescott, AZ

A High School Freshman

We say, "I love you," and she kisses my cheek,
Then she was gone.
My mom's car vanishing down the street,
Like a plane being covered by billowy clouds.
There was nowhere to go but straight ahead.
Ahead into a row of halls, like the rows of corn fields never ending
Like a sea made up of people, I'm afraid to drown.
I am a freshman, a freshman I am.
Am I scared, lost, or afraid to frown?
Can I get used to what's going 'round?
Students to the left and students to the right,
Students judging and students uptight.
I made it safe to class, feeling like a lost kitten that found its way home.
I see a familiar face; yes, a familiar face, now I know I am not alone.
Days go by, weeks go by, months roll by,
Time goes by;
I am not scared, I am not lost, I am not afraid.
I did not drown nor did I frown.
I am okay.
I am a freshman, a freshman I am.

Vivian Diaz
Harlingen, TX

If

If plants were given the gift of speech
If birds could talk instead of sing
If water foamed with words aflow
If animals were verbal with ideas aglow
I know the words they would beseech
And those words are: to live in peace

If man was but a passing thought
If intelligence was prized instead of bought
If love was sacred above all else
If respect was given instead of dealt
If heart to heart was given not taken
Our Earth would be God's paradise in making

Jill Gomez
Sacramento, CA

My sister and I were born in Deluth, Minnesota and moved to California when we were eight and nine years old. We lived with our father and stepmom til we got married and went to live our own lives. I started writing poetry at the age of seventeen in high school and when I was in my early thirties, had two poems published in books. One poem titled "The Eyes" is a spiritual poem and the other poem is titled "Sonnet of Love." I continue to write and am inspired by events in my life and others'.

What a Wonderful God Is He

Creator of the universe and all that dwells within
Bled and died on Calvary to save us from our sin
Glorious, magnificent, a wonderful God is He
Healed the sick, set the captives free
Raised the dead, walked on the sea
Glorious, magnificent, a wonderful God is He
Five thousand hungry souls He fed
With two little fishes and five loaves of bread
Glorious, magnificent, a wonderful God is He
What a wonderful God, a wonderful God
What a wonderful God is He

"And His name shall be called wonderful, counselor, the mighty God,
the everlasting Father, the prince of peace." -Isaiah 9:6

Joan Rivers
Jamaica, NY

*I was raised and nourished in the word of God by my wonderful grandfather,
pastor, and founder of our church. This way of life is all in my spirit. We
were taught as children to extend love, "Thank you, Jesus." God blessed
me to write these words of encouragement and thanksgiving, without Him
I could not do it. I realize God has chosen me to share His holy word and
through this I remain under His direction, prepared to do what he has me to
do. "Giving thanks always for all things unto God and the Father in the name
of our Lord Jesus Christ." -Ephesians 5:20*

Homeless Monologue

Solid orange bricks, an abandoned structure. Is there room or is it wasted?
Watch out for the broken-down shopping carts. The windshield is
clean now.
Next right—center for warming straight ahead.
(What exactly is spare change?)
The land of opportunity surrounds me with signs and wonders.
Whatever it takes and I'm not too proud to beg.
In fact, "will work for food."
Shorter days and longer nights.
It's time to fall back into the ruts of winter cold.
Yes, I am cold too.
I might even freeze to death alone outside a high school
Where students study the great land of America.
Everyone wants to live in America.
Shelters, public assistance, welfare
Nothing more or (possibly) much less.
A lukewarm cup of soup and a tattered, soiled blanket.
Please sir, I want more!
Never mind. Forgot my place, know where I belong.
A cozy, dirty alley, a warm snow-covered overpass. Choices.
Rest a while. It's safe. Isn't it? I always sleep here,
there,
somewhere,
nowhere.

G. A. Ausby
Oak Park, MI

Merry Sunshine

If I can bask in the golden radiance of your smile
If the sparkle of laughter can be mine for a while
If to be with you can ever be my choice, then my happiness can know
no bounds
For I will have found a garden, an Eden no less
A place where whirling merry-go-rounds are forever spreading the
magic music of happiness
A place where you are

Vince Loerich
Denver, CO

Hope

Sometimes I wish my life would just end
I tell you, with this message I send.

You protest against my despair,
but I act like I don't even care.

Hope is knowing what to do,
hope is having someone there for you.

I feel like I can cope
because you give me hope

Katy Stephenson
Imperial Beach, CA

Lines

Two white lines, two yellow lines
and sometimes a dotted line direct
my way. My tired, bloodshot eyes
stare trance-like, through the
evening mist, as my wet tires slap
in a hypnotic rhythm.

These lines, straight and curved
and always side by side, direct
me through tobacco fields, barns
with colts and mares, one-pump
gas stations, and a small white
house with red geraniums, a
white-washed fence and a sign that
says, *Antiques, come in.*

The lines keep going, mile after mile,
interrupted by an occasional yellow
square with a maverick line,
alerting me to new directions.

And suddenly, the lines have ended
and I am alone, with no direction.

Patricia Botkin
Clarksville, TN

My Treasure

There is a little work of art
That all my life I'll treasure
The art is by a two-year-old
—Love for her I can't measure.

Never told her that I loved her,
Didn't watch her in her play,
Only knew her from some photos
'Cause we lived so far away.

My arms always ached to hold her
And to hear her little voice,
But someday when I'm in Heaven,
Then together, we'll rejoice.

I talked oft' to God about her—
Every morning, every night—
She was blessed with wondrous parents
Who did everything just right.

All her suffering now is over
And her pain is gone away
For she has returned to Heaven,
Angels called for her today.

Her painting I will always love
And with it I'll never part,
Each time that I admire it
I will hug her in my heart.

Agnes Steede
Independence, MO

Gift to a Friend

You gave me a little hope in life. I'm so grateful to you. You gave me your friendship without a hesitation. You've given me so much, yet I've given you so little. You will go your way, I shall go my way, but with the pleasure of having known a person like you. You and I, we make a team in a way. We are two persons in pain, but struggling to overcome it every single day. That is why I give you these simple gifts as a token of our friendship.

Brown is your color, red is mine, and they join together to complement one another. Your brown is my strength, red is my beauty and yellow the coming of a bright day for both of us. The green is our hope that everything will come true. Blue stands for the intensity of my words.

Guillermina E. Corporan
Lyons, GA

Holiday in Hawaii

Sand and surf and skies so blue, what a lovely place to be,
Soaking up the sunny rays, around the pool or salty sea.
From Vancouver to Honolulu, a pleasant five-hour flight,
Pick up a car and travel to the Makaha condo site.
Now ten days stretch before us to enjoy every sight and sound,
So I would like to tell you how we got around:

The Dole Plantation, Kodak Hula Show and the Aloha Tower,
Then to Hooters for lunch at the appropriate hour
The spectacular Punch Bowl, the Arizona Memorial, too,
Have a special place in history at Pearl Harbor, Oahu.
A jazz concert at University Courtyard, enjoyable in the open air;
"Miss Saigon" at the Blaisdell Center, we were happy to be there.

Banyan trees spread their leaves like an umbrella to the sky,
Colorful flowers, birds that sing, stately peacocks that cry.
From fiery-red sunsets that set to the dark of night
And rise hours later to a day clear and bright.
Limos long and lovely, you see them everywhere,
And precious little trolleys—they'll take you here and there.

Fresh pineapple and papaya, a real treat to savor;
So juicy and delicious, they have a different flavor.
Red dirt so strange to see from ancient volcanic action,
The breaking waves upon the shore, a surfer-watching attraction.
All these impressions come to mind, events that gave me pleasure,
I keep within my memory, to treasure at my leisure.

Winnifred Langham
Kelowna, BC

Words come easily to me when inspired by events—like my trip to Hawaii, a beautiful state. I am eighty-eight years old and live in Kelowna, BC, CA. Some writings of mine have appeared in a local community newspaper and other publications. I just enjoy putting words together. With a family of six children, seven grandchildren and three great-grandchildren, and all those years behind me, I have many stories to tell in verse.

Restless Without

Red, yellow and pink flowers bloom
Vines wither across the room
Lying awake with red, brown eyes
It gets harder and harder to sleep at night
So dead, so mellow, a knock from whom?
Your constant dream or ancient doom
Stumbling slowly to bliss or fright
While thoughtfully moving to turn on the light
It may be the one that fills you with gloom
You hope it's the man that makes your heart move
Prepare for the outcome, build up your might
Answer it wisely, prepare for a fight
Open to find null but a bright white moon
But, then you feel arms that brighten your mood
It's him; it's the one, the love of your life
So, come off to bed, we'll sleep easy tonight!

Natasha Zuri Springer
York, PA

Special Person

Wind and water, earth and sky, a
perfect moment flowing by; air and
ocean, sand and sky, a perfect moment
just begun

A sunbeam through your window, a
thought that makes you smile and
reminders all day long of how
special you are to those who
comfort you, encourage you and
love you

Always sharing greatest joys and
deepest hurts, revealing your wildest
dreams and secrets of the soul with
heartfelt words, it's sharing the stories
of your past and your hopes for
tomorrow

It's experiencing the tears, the
laughter and the craziness of life
with someone who understands so
much so it's with someone like
you

Ginette Dowinski
Winnipeg, MB

My Angel, My Daughter, My Friend

Thank you for making my life worthwhile.
Thank you for giving me reason to smile.
Thank you for making me feel that I'm the "best."
Thank you for not making me suffer the "empty nest."

Through laughter, fun, tears and strife,
Thank you for putting children in my life.
You have such integrity, intelligence and grace,
There's so much goodness and beauty in your lovely face.

You have such compassion in your loving heart,
You always have had, right from the start.
You are so good in all that you do,
That's why when I grow up, I want to be just like you.

I feel so honored to be your mother;
If I could choose, I'd choose no other.
Our times together are far too few,
My life is truly blessed because of you.

I love the fun and laughter we share,
Sometimes we really are quite the pair.
By your side is where I want to be,
I'm so thankful God sent you to me.

My child, remember when things get you down,
Your mother's love is deep and profound.
That's why for you I've composed this poem,
For whereever you are that is my home.

So darling, this I will say again:
My love for you will never end.
Your loving mother

Iris E. Kerns
St. Joseph, MO

It Will Always Stay

My house was built
from the strong,
working hands of
Hephaestus. But
was made my home by Hestia, and always will be in my heart.
Zeus might send storms, strike his lightning, and have his thunder
boom. But it will always stay. Poseidon might send his waves rushing.
But it will always stay. Ares might try to bring an army attacking, or guns
firing. But it will always stay. Boreas, Eurus, Notus, and Zephyrs might bring
their winds together to sway my house. But it will always stay.
Hermes could try to steal things or play some tricks. But it will
always stay. Artemis could send her wild hunt or animals come
and attack. But it will always stay. Apollo might send a plague
or block the sun from my house. But it will always stay. Athena
could bring welfare, and Demeter might make our yard go pale.
Dionysus would bring madness and Chaos would bring chaos.
But it will always stay. Penthos or Penthus could bring grief and
mourning. Plutus might not come to our help and let us have
financial troubles. But it will always stay. Now that this poem
is nearing the end, I hope you understand how dear my house is
to me. I grew up there and had many important experiences, too.
Hopefully, it will do what I've been saying and always stay.

Olivia Revels
Beloit, WI

The Lady Living in a Paper Box

There's a light over in a distant corner
No houses, not even buildings
But there's a lady in that paper box

It's cold, it's raining, why?
Why is she sleeping in that paper box?
No stove to cook her food
Nowhere to take a bath
But there's a lady in that paper box

She has a towel to lay her head on
And a sponge to take her bath
The water from a hole that's outside the paper box

We have so much but yet we mumble and groan
But the lady lives in a paper box

Amen

Joan Dorman
Chadbourn, NC

My inspiration to write "The Lady Living in a Paper Box" was living in Washington, DC, working around the homeless and seeing people eating out of trash cans, sleeping in boxes, and lying on the streets over heating vents to keep warm—nowhere to go or lay their heads, dirty, hungry, but still were smiling. This hurt my heart. We have so much, but still want more. I saw how God took care of the homeless. I never saw the homeless sick. So with the help of God's love in my life, I composed this poem.

After the Valley

Coming out of the valley. . .yes, it is so sweet
The offense on my soul, ended not in defeat.
Life will toss you and turn you. . .yes, even upside down
But hold on tight this time. . .you're not the clown.
Wipe those tears and suck it up, they say
No. . .not too easy. . .who cares anyway?
Just go through your difficulties one step at a time
Soon, higher and higher the mountains you climb.
For you know without a doubt, clearing is soon
And furthermore. . .you may be even singing a tune.
A tune from the heart is always the best.
Try it sometime
It'll separate you from the rest.
The rest you know may have hope you see
But some of the rest. . .I choose not to be.
I am who I am. . .this I will say
Nobody is always perfect, anyway.

Carol Emmett
Canton, MI

Remembering

This captivating love of mine
Is looking fit and feeling fine.
Four decades have gone by so fast,
She marvels how the time has passed.
Now as she walks along the beach
The breakers surge within her reach.
The tide is rising as it flows
Up through the sand between her toes.
And when she lays beside the pool
The gentle breezes keep her cool
While sunlight leaves a gentle trace
Of tan upon her lovely face.
Her eyes are closed though not in sleep
And memories begin to creep
As she reflects upon her life
And all the years she's been my wife.
We've shared so much throughout the years,
A lot of joys, some tender tears.
As time unfolds for us, I pray
We'll be together every day.

Loyal E. Babcock
San Diego, CA

On our 40th anniversary my wife Selma and I went to Hawaii. We spent some time on Oahu at Waikiki Beach and some time on Maui. While we walked along the beaches and took a dip in the clear blue water I was inspired to write this poem about the beautiful lady I had married forty years before. Over the years we had two handsome and successful boys. And then their lovely wives blessed us with four beautiful granddaughters. A fifth granddaughter was born prematurely and died in infancy, but we feel blessed with a great-grandchild on the way.

Sandy Hook

Friday, December 14, 2012 at 9:30 AM, in Newtown, Connecticut
twenty-seven lights in our world were snuffed out!
For no reason at all, twenty were just babies,
between five and seven years old, with many maybes
in their lives foretold. . all taken away as
the gunman takes aim, all their futures, gone!
What a waste, what a shame. . as I sit and cry
for all the families' pain! But at least we know
that the demon is dead, the coward shot. . .
himself in the head! After I heard this news,
I sat crying in disbelief. . the wind started
blowing. . really hard, dark clouds formed. . .
in the sky. . then. . burst forth with. . a pouring
rain! The universe mourning all who were
slain! Such senseless violence in the world
today, for the ones left behind, I pray, as
their loved ones' lights ascend to Heaven. . .
Please look to the night sky, as they shine
down on us all! A blood-red sunset on this
day. . .

Lorraine Vaughan
San Diego, CA

Life's Journey

Life is like a swirling whirlwind
Circling first this way and then that way
Starting from the day we are born
And ending the day we complete our journey

At birth, our parents nurture us
Taught by them along with our teachers
And in time, we become the person we are

Laugh, love, give and we live
We cherish the beauty around us
Our bodies change with age
Our souls are nurtured
Awaiting the day in which it departs
And goes to a better place
Where it will live on forever

Thank God for the lifelong journey
Preparing us to be like Him
In the heavenly hereafter

Carolyn Morris
Waynesburg, PA

The Love of My Life, My Rose

In the fertile loam of my heart there lies
A garden where the love of my life grows,
Where the winged thoughts of my mind flies
To pay homage to the love of my life, my Rose.

I lost myself in pools of hazel green,
While in my breast sleeping passion arose,
I found myself in the most beautiful eyes I've ever seen,
Created just for me, the love of my life, my Rose.

Only God can create two for each other to be complete,
In this way His love for each of us He shows
In shortness of breath and heartbeats that are fleet,
To love each other as we loved, the love of my life, my Rose.

Her silky highlighted brunette tresses,
Scented like a sweet, sweet savor to my nose,
Her figure divine in the simplest dresses,
Beauty incarnate is the love of my life, my Rose.

Love is complicated in all its simplicity,
For centuries romanticized in silver-tongued prose,
Many have expressed their heartfelt felicity
For the one they love, like I love the love of my life, my Rose.

You might say I am a fool for love,
But I know one reaps bountifully what he sows,
And poor is he who does not know the depth of the love
We felt, me and the love of my live, my Rose.

David M. Young
Aurora, CO

Summer's End

In late September there came a cool breeze
Sooner or later it was going to freeze

A touch of fall was in the air
Means winter's coming, better get prepared

Made a list of things to do
Not too many, only a few

Seal the cracks around the windows and doors
Vegetables from the garden put away and stored

Roll up the hose and rake up the leaves
Get out the brush and clean the chimney

The boards on the deck need painted red
The lawn and garden tools stored in the shed

Then towards evening came a bit of a chill
Got out some steaks and fired up the grill

Invited over some family and friends
Summer had definitely come to an end

Got things squared away with some time to spare
Went and sat down in my easy chair

A little fatigued but my list was done
Took a nap by the fire, let winter come

Lyle Jensen
Idaho Falls, ID

One Summer

The curtains smack me playfully,
Dancing with the cool October air.
As the sun streams across your face,
I think back to the first summer
We had alone together.

We were gardening for hours,
Singing made-up melodies
Because you believed the corn would grow sweeter.
We would cool off in the glacier-fed stream
That ran through your backyard.

I waded for hours
Trying to find the gold you told me was there.
Ten empty, purple, pruney fingers—
Finally admitted defeat.
You smiled at me with wise eyes,
Next time, you promised.

The curtain tickled my arm,
Bringing me back.
Staring into your eyes
Framed in narrow black plastic.
Gazing at your picture,
Wishing Grandpa and I
Could go panning for gold once more.

Alyssa Salandi
Columbia Falls, MT

When I Say Goodbye

It is sad to think of my last farewell
  and the things I will leave behind
And I hope that some of them will stay around
  for a long, long time

I hope the sweet bay down in the swamp
  will always bloom in the spring
And that it will saturate the breeze with sweetness
  for those who will pass after me

And I hope that the old turkey gobbler
  among snowy dogwood blossoms will ever be found
And that he will electrify the early spring mornings
  with a haunting and primitive sound

And I hope that the bobwhite will always be ready
  to pipe out his wonderful tune
To assure us that the world is in order
  on a perfect day in June

And I hope that the wild, black muscadine grapes
  will always be there in September
To give to others the sweet fragrant taste
  that I so fondly remember

And I hope that the longleaf pine
  will always sing in the wind
For the creatures and folks who will pass this way
  where I will not pass again

Joseph R. McDonald
Hoffman, NC

Laurel for Maria

The limberness of your body stirs up admiration,
Your professional knowledge—respect,
Your thoughtfulness arouses fascination,
Your mind and beauty shines.

Your gentleness is uniting people
With the elegance you support activity,
Your honesty, which kindles envy,
Engrafts confidence in people's minds.

How do you do this, that day or night
You are not ejecting worries out the door?
What do I think about it? My answer is short:
Your greatness is rooted in the depth of your soul.

For all of this you deserve thanks,
Love, appreciation, the best fate;
Your person is like morning star beam,
What fights down evil in man.

Kazimierz Oskedra
Carlsbad, CA

Nice White Woman

He was on the bus already
As we sat where we could
I across and you behind
That poor tattered-clad soul
Full of smiles and greetings bold
No one answering in kind
He was a simple-minded man
From a very friendly mold

I saw you speaking to that man
As you tried to be so nice
I was very proud of you
And I surely understand
You thought you were past it
Until he reached out his hand
To say thank you and goodbye
As would any gentleman

Then you winced and offered yours
You shook in a friendly way
He left on a note of grace. . .
You will not me convince
'Nor my opinion sway
As you glanced at your hand
Did you really think that color, black,
Would somehow seep into your pores?

Anita L. Ellsworth
Florence, AZ

I am a seventy-six-year-old desert dweller who has never rode a city bus. This was a first-time adventure for me. One of my favorite pastimes is watching people. On that bus was a lively little black man. He was mentally challenged and very unkept. After many tries to talk to a friendly person, he caught the smiling eyes of the young woman seated across from me. She became his captive audience for several blocks. As he got up to leave the bus, he reached out for her hand. That moment is frozen in time for me. May God richly bless those two precious souls.

Our Lost Word

There are words to express our every emotion
Words to describe our every notion
There are words to translate our thoughts, ideas,
and imagination
Words to be used for every explanation
We have words to interpret our dreams, the
universe, and the abstract
Words in our everyday lives to keep us intact
But to say that I love you or am in love with you
does not make my heart ring clear
For these words once spoken, like mist, can
disappear
There are words such as *cherish, desire,* or *adore*
which hit their mark
But again, once uttered they can vanish like a
spark
So I believe, to truly understand what you mean
to me I can only use a word that must have been
lost
Somewhere in time, into the stars, it found itself
tossed
But in silence embraced together, if we listen
closely within our hearts can always be heard
The beauty and the power of our lost word

Gregory N. Rocco
Cornwall-on-Hudson, NY

When Your Heart Longs to Soar

"It's hard to keep your feet grounded when your heart longs to fly," it's
been said. Feet destined to stay on earth, but a heart came with wings
at its birth.
Still those wings will grow and fly until
the human learns the selfish part of them must die.
It's hard to keep your feet grounded when your heart longs to fly.
It's hard to keep your feet down when the wind calls your heart away.
It's hard to stay when the spirit says, "Fly with me today."
Your feet may be stubborn, but your heart ignores its pleas and in an
instant the heart spreads its wings.
It's hard to keep your feet down when the wind calls your heart away.
It's hard to keep your feet grounded when your heart longs to soar.
People on the ground look up to you flying. They call out to you as if
they are dying.
They say, "Come back down to earth!" They are insisting as they say,
"Your dreams are too high to reach, come back down with us and stay."
You keep flying though, not heeding the people below, knowing that
they too once knew, "It is hard to keep your feet grounded when your
heart longs to soar."

Elisabeth Grace Stanley
China Spring, TX

*This poem started as most of my writing does: as a word or phrase. The
phrase was: "it is hard to keep your feet grounded when your heart longs
to soar." The phrase came from the belief that everyone has a dream to do
something awesome, but some people tell you that it is too far fetched or
impossible. Nothing is impossible. If people want to stick with what is safe,
then that is their choice, but it doesn't have to be yours. My favorite quote is
from Benjamin Franklin: "if you cannot read good literature, then write good
literature." Courage and Godspeed, knights of the pen!*

The Superiority of God

When human life began,
God created one woman and one man.
Every generation
is the offspring of the two.

The people in this world
who acknowledge this fact are very few.
Let's spread the word
and teach them from whence they came.

We are all made in the image of God,
and we are all the same.
God made this beautiful universe
for all humans to inhabit.

He put us all in different places
with different statues and different faces.
Though there are some
that think they are superior
and all others are so very small,
but they tend to forget
that God created and loves us all.

In Christ there are no minorities,
so no one should feel inferior.
For only the Almighty God
holds the title of being superior.

Melba L. Stewart
Lancaster, CA

Jennifer Corrin

You are the daughter I received the
day that you were born,
and I just want to thank you
for all that you've become.

You filled our home with joyous notes
when your fingers touched the keys.
You cooked and baked, made arts and crafts
with which any mother would be pleased.

The choices you have made so far
in life and talent and friends
are some of the finest
preparing you for the challenges that lie ahead.

I thank the Lord each and every day
for giving me this angel.
The woman that I cherish now
was once the baby I cradled.

I will always love you, Jennifer.

Corrine Simi
Apple Valley, MN

The Smallest Angel

Once there was an angel
With tiny wings aglow
Who sat upon a big white cloud
And watched it begin to snow.

Her halo was a circle of gold
Upon her tiny head
That shined and made the whole world bright
As the stories once had said.

Her hair was long and hung in curls
And upon her shoulders streamed,
And crystal snowflakes mingled there
As if it had been dreamed.

She looked up high into the sky,
A shooting star was there;
She began to dance around
Without a single care.

And then when night began to fall,
So sleepy she did seem,
She lay her head down upon the white mound
And let the twilight gleam.

Wanda C. Campbell
Iuka, MS

Song of Songs

The night brings tears to my eyes
It is of joy, for poetry itself visits my heart
There is perhaps up in the skies, a brand new poem
Cherubim to Earth has just arrived

The night sings softly, a new song
It is of love, the sweetest melody I have ever heard
Tender, sublime *song of songs*
God gave me a son!
This is a holy night in the whole world

The night has painted my soul with his smile
It is pure gold; it shines just like no other ever will
All within me, has it all
Light, peace, love, son. . .

Oh, life, I celebrate, for happy I am!

Pablo Hugo Penalver
Ridgewood, NY

The immense joy of having a son makes one feel like it is possible to fly like a bird and soar through the air towards the skies. Then for a moment I closed my eyes, visited the moon, flew back home, and at that hour in which it is not daylight nor is it yet nighttime. This poem was born "Song of Songs" which I've dedicated to my beloved son Huguito.

Terrific Twix

I can hear the crinkle of the wrapper as I open it to see the
beautiful long bar of chocolate with caramel flavor in the inside.
I can taste the texture of the Twix as it enters my mouth.
Your chocolate is so yummy,
Your caramel is so yummy,
Your cookie crunch is so yummy,
And now you are in my tummy!
It's heaven!
It's like I drank a crunchy cup of hot chocolate.
I feel it melt in my mouth as I taste the sensation over my
taste buds.
I could eat a thousand of them,
They taste so good I just want to savor their flavor.

Deidre Medley
North Pole, FL

*When I was in eighth grade my language arts teacher gave me a poem
assignment. The topic of the poem was our favorite candy. Along with the
poem, we also had to make a bigger version of our candy out of paper, tissue
paper, and newspaper. She wanted us to find a creative way to include the
poem into the project. I made it so when you opened the wrapper, two bars
of paper came out and the poem was glued to it. I ended up getting an A on
the project. It was also displayed for everyone to see.*

I Love You Because

It's good to do God's work
He doesn't expect a lifestyle rut to hold us back
We need a sense of direction to see
It's okay if our faith levels differ,
      to recognize our need
Is He pleased with us, to use talent given we?
I love you because
I love in a different sort of way
Support with tolerance from you to me
As you lift me up with love, let me be
      who I am
Look inside my heart of love
No attendant paid for how the outside
      appeared to be
 Even if you're bored with me, still you
      share my company
A reason to love you, because

Doris Lambert
Winchester, VA

Ode to Sandy Sue

When I was a twinkle in my daddy's eye and the Lord said it's time to go,
I looked over in the corner on a little pink cloud and saw a brand new
batch of dough.
I said, "Lord, what's that?" and He smiled and said, "Why, it's a brand
new baby sister,
I'm making her for you," and He stroked her head and then He bent
and kissed her.
"Can't I just take her with me," I asked right then, "since I'm already
going that way?"
He said, "Not just yet, I'm working on her and she'll be perfect some day."
Well, I waited around and while I waited I grew and finally came the day.
There was lots of commotion, everyone was in motion, and then I
heard someone say,
"Well look at this perfect baby girl, I wonder what name will do?"
I said, "The Lord sent her down to follow me around and her name is
Sandy Sue."
He said she'd be perfect but I wasn't sure, she was a wrinkled and red
little sister,
but since she was the only one I had, I bent down and kissed her.
She started to grow and follow me around and sometimes she caused
me trouble.
She was always chewing bubble gum and blowing a monstrous bubble,
the end of her nose was always black, and she drove the poor dog crazy,
And when it was time to go to school she could be a little lazy.
She walked in her sleep or slipped off from home and went to visit the
neighbors,
and sometimes I thought, if they'd keep her a while, they might be doing
a favor.
But her big brown eyes were always on me and they melted my heart a
little.
Was she perfect yet? I didn't know, I was somewhere in the middle.
But as time would have it, she grew up one day into a perfect little sister
and I finally knew how lucky I was and I bent down and kissed her

Sharon R. Smith
Charleston, WV

*I wrote this poem for my sister, Sandra Sue Smith Walker, on Valentine's
Day. She is my only sibling and we are always there for each other. I wanted
her to know how very special she is to me, so this poem is dedicated to her
and in memory of our parents.*

Comes and Goes

Does death come often. . everyday
or does it come to one person
then move onto the next?
Is death the end
or just the beginning of a new life?

I wonder, is your soul alive or dead?
Do bones turn to ash or rise above with you?
Does God expect the unexpected
or is he prepared for what's coming?

Is death a crime or a gift?
Who knows where these bodies go.
Is death a sign?
Should we be happy or sad?

Is death the end of happiness
or more excitement?
Death is a mystery.

Ava Tulipano
Bronx, NY

I'm a student who enjoys to write. It has been a passion of mine since I was little. My inspirations are basically everything around me. I'm a dancer and a former cheerleader. What is pretty cool is that it was my grandmother's idea to enter my poem. My poem was originally from my fifth-grade yearbook. Basically, I'm an original looking to share my talents. I'm not afraid to share my opinions because they may come to good use. I have high expectations for myself and hope to achieve my dreams in the future.

Night

The moon in silvery glow suspended
Has no clouds to darken her glory,
No wind in the heavens so splendid,
The silence can tell such a story.

It tells of toils finally ended,
Of creatures gladly quiet and still,
Of chatter and noise that's rescinded
Quiet magic that enchants with a thrill.

Angela Griffin
Martinsville, VA

Holiday Out

Holidays are a *disruption*,
They are full of *strife*.
They alter the flow of *life*,
Of *mail, banking* and *trash collection*.
Death does not take a *holiday*.
Nature does not have any *say*.

So why should *we*?

Except to *boost the economy!*

Cliff O'Connell
Granada Hills, CA

Reminiscing

When I was young, my mother would say,
Things were not what they are today.
People were quieter and they would walk far,
They never dreamed of a plane or a car.

A stroll in the woods, a walk in the rain
Or watching the coming of the new choo-choo train.
For pleasure, a visit, a stroll or a chat—
Not dancing or gambling or things such as that.
A fiddler's convention, a fair, and the like,
For these, across country the people would hike.
Or into the buggies the family would go
And off to church—fair weather or snow—
To worship and sing and pray and shout.
Their old-time religion was something to talk about.

About seven o'clock and sometimes before,
They'd wait for the sound of a knock on the door,
For someone was sure to visit tonight;
The moon was shining, and the stars were bright.
And visitors and neighbors were welcome at our door
For everyone had completed his own little chore.

Now our dreams are all over, and we come with a start
To the present when people are so far apart.
Your next door neighbor is a stranger to you,
And one never talks with ones in the next pew.
No wonder mother would sigh when she would say,
Things used to be different from what they are today.

Alease Wright Lambert
Mount Airy, NC

Music Haiku

Music all around.
The playing is perfection.
It's grateful music.

Trinity K. Jackson
St Augustine, FL

Blue Fields

This day
As I wandered
Through a field of blue,
A field colored blue
By wild blue lupines
Blooming,
All the tiny
Pale-blue butterflies
That had been dining there
Rose up
And fluttered around me,
Welcoming me
Into their blue world

Shirley Voll
Baraboo, WI

The Bride

A lovely bride. . .
   gliding by like a dove on an updraft.
   Air-brushed make-up pure perfection.
   Do I know her?
   I did.
   When sun alone colored her complexion.

Soft hands. . .
   clutching the fragrant bouquet so tightly.
   The fingertips—sparkling as her eyes.
   Do I recognize them?
   Ah, yes!
   Little fingers bearing many a surprise!

Slender feet. . .
   wearing perfect peacock feather shoes
   peek out beneath the lacy hem.
   The same chubby little toes
   digging for shells in the sand?
   Yes, I remember them!

In her heart. . .
   love.
   Some things never change!

Susan M. Baker
St. Augustine, FL

Healing Broken Wings

Scream and shout
Breathe in, breathe out
As your eyes raise
Focus your gaze
Straighten your stature
Ignore their laughter
Take a stand against the wrong
You are the one who is strong
You don't need them
They aren't real friends
You will go on
So sing your song
Run fast, jump high
You will be the one to fly

Haley Salak
Waymart, PA

As a quiet student in high school, I often find myself observing the actions of others. Some of my observations are not those of which I would have hoped to see. In a world where bullying has become a major controversy, I find it unfortunate that I still see it in schools. My poem, "Healing Broken Wings," is my way to speak out against bullying and speak to those who are bullied. My hope is that the message it conveys will give off a sense of courage to keep moving forward.

Home

This house I enter now is bare,
the rooms are strangely still.
There is no step upon the stair,
no flower blooming on the windowsill.
No clock is ticking the hours away,
there is no need for time,
nothing dwells within these walls
but memories of mine.
I close the door and walk away,
my eyes are filled with tears.
I can't return, but I won't forget
this house, my home for many years.

Millie Kolp
Ashland, OH

In the past after visiting my vacant, childhood home, I wrote this poem to express my emotions. I write poetry when life challenges me to understand its mysteries. My family consists of a daughter, two sons, six grandchildren and seven great-grandchildren. I enjoy family, music, and gardening and am eighty-nine. God's blessings to all.

A Valentine's Day Walk Home

Off the bus,
Thinking, thinking, thinking.
Up the driveway,
Trudging and thinking, trudging and thinking.
In the house,
Parents are looking, looking, looking.
Those earlier, happier eleven Valentine's Days rattling inside me like
Pennies in a tin Band-Aid box,
Making so much noise, too much noise.
Parents discuss problems in school,
Yelling, screaming, yelling, screaming.
My face droops like the edge of a waterfall,
Sadness, sadness, sadness.
Up the stairs,
Stomping my feet like I am three,
Wishing the day's events would disappear into the sky, like a runaway
balloon.

Alex Schwalb
Jeffersonville, NY

I'm a proud thirteen-year-old! I live in the rural area of Jeffersonville, New York. I'm currently going into the eighth grade in the wonderful Sullivan West. Yes, I know what you're thinking: an eighth grader in high school? Well, in my school district, there's just an elementary school and a high school! I play soccer, basketball, and baseball. I play the alto saxophone, too. I have a sister and six pets. What inspired my poem was the events of this year's Valentine's Day. That's me in a nutshell!

Stallions of the Sky

Small, effervescent creatures of flight
Wings so sheer you could see through them
Quick to appear and darting off
Up, around and down, here and there
seeming to appear everywhere at once
so many of them too numerous to even count
I remember watching their delightful ballet in the sky
A symphony bursting forth
with amazing voices of
contraltos and sopranos
gloriously fit together in a song of flight
And yet heckling you as if to say,
Catch me if you can!
I remember being so little,
attempting to reach up and catch one
I always thought that if I were still enough
one of them would land on my fingertips
They didn't
When I was young it never occurred to me
that one day they would vanish
And today I saw just one,
wondering where they all went to
and if it, too, like all the others
would disappear and be gone forever
My dragonflies, my stallions, my symphony
of the skies

Denise Mills
Oroville, CA

A Beautiful Day

The dawn has come with its sun so bright
you shield your eyes with such wondrous delight
As you watch the bright rays bounce
from tree to tree,
You realize no day can be better than today.
Then you look up to the heaven above—
you see dark clouds forming about.
Soon the radiant sun is gone,
now rain dropping where the sun had once shown.
The air is now cool and all is so wet,
the smell of rich earth comes with each breath.
And as you watch soon you'll with glory see
the sun again shining there among the trees.
With rain drops glistening one by one,
what a beautiful sight the day has become.
Now all too soon this day has gone by,
with moon and stars now traveling all through the sky,
their bright light shining, such a wonder to see.
Then as you reflect on this day with its glory now past,
You can look forward to the next day
with its beauty once again forever to last.

Elizabeth Parker
Bridgeton, NC

The Sea of Life

I sailed across the sea of life toward a promised land
But then the storms of trials came—my ship got out of hand!
The waves were rough; "I'm lost," I cried, "my ship is tossed and blown!"
But then I heard the Savior's voice: "Fresh courage, you're not alone!"

It seemed that steady was the wheel against that fearsome blast,
and I no longer was afraid of losing life and mast.
I prayed aloud: "Just show the way that I may pass the test!"
And He responded willingly and helped me do the rest.

Now when the winds subsided and blue skies were showing through,
I took the wheel alone again and charted course anew!
Oh, now I know. . when "storms of life" on crests of waves do ride,
I'll never sink or lose my ship with the Savior as my guide!

Charlene A. Newell
Draper, UT

The Mastectomy

You and I were intimate,
Complete.
One was never without the other.
Separation! Who could imagine?

We lived in full honor, respect and trust
of what each brought to the other,
Serving the whole of life.

When the knife came
There was no time to say goodbye.

The witness self—
Observed
The blood flow into the sponges.

The stitching seemed easy enough,
Woven into
The surgeon's conversation of the day.

The exquisite feminine form over the left heart
Was sent to the lab,
Diagnosed,
And thrown into hazardous waste.

Today,
Tears of remembrance
Flow
For our once-upon-a-time
Together.

Loci S. Yonder
San Diego, CA

Poetry was my solace and delight in childhood. It never failed to offer a stretch into the possibility of some new space of truth and wisdom. It helped and fascinated me. I felt a deep strength I wanted to know. Through words and rhythm, I was transported into pioneering with permission to enter unknown spaces. The balance offered to the stress and demands of my childhood was profound. This momentum, however, was eclipsed in the growing-up process. Only when stopped through illness did I return to poetry, this time to write, to say, to listen, and to express.

Something More

People always ask, "Why is there such darkness?
Why is there such evil?"
Without darkness, light serves no purpose.
Light would be so common that it wouldn't
really be light anymore, would it?
It would just be a mediocre, always-existing,
dull status quo that would leave us
begging on our knees for more.
And that's what darkness is for, to remind us
that we want something more.
And that's what light is, it's our *something more*.
Something more than you can ever imagine,
something so great and selfless that it gave
itself for us, even though we could never even
begin to deserve it.
My Savior is my light, my Savior is my
something more.

Madeline Smith
Mansfield, TX

Timeless Avenues of Life

Time to laugh, time to spend
Time to plan, time to expend
Refreshing time childhood sends

Life's a battle, newborns wail
Marriage tries, adventurer's sail
Deep sea depth still to scale

Staring at a star so far, so pale
A plane that leaves a smoky trail
Which man will travel so to regale

Some to brag, some to be meek
Different objectives to find, to seek
Knowledge of mind still to speak

Ages roll, time grows nigh
Farewell to dreams, we sleep, we die
Eternity is timeless, we sigh, we cry
Goodbye, goodbye, goodbye, goodbye

Lola Pennington
North Wilkesboro, NC

Last Light

The day is done—
The setting sun prepares its evening show.
What colors will He paint tonight?
That only God can know.

His hand produces reds and golds
That turn the clouds to flame,
Then spears of sunlight stab the sky
Avoiding earthly claim.

I find peace in every sunset
Far away from the worldly rush.
There is no "same old, same old"
When the master wields His brush.

Some day soon I'll slip away
Beyond that setting sun
To begin my journey down the "road"
Now that earthly tasks are done.

The steps I take along the "road"
Aren't measured by the mile,
But by every joyous greeting
And each warm, familiar smile.

Friendly hands now gently guide me
Toward the place where I will be
Immersed in that spectrum of color
Blended by the great artist for me.

Barbara Isern
Mapleton Depot, PA

The first three stanzas of "Last Light" were composed in April, 2012 during one of my daily "sunset watches." I phoned my dear friend of forty-four years in Arizona to share it with her. She loved it and asked me to send her a copy. I did so with a note that said, "Maybe down the road, we will walk together and thank God personally." On Mother's Day, 2012 my friend, M.P., at the age of ninety-one went peacefully to be with the Lord. The last three stanzas were written the following day. I miss you, Marion.

Everybody's Shadow Is the Same Color

Those who would ever preach to deny
The basic freedom of others,
Create horrendous turmoil in our lives.
They neglect the concept of sister and brother,
And that everybody's shadow is the same color.

Let those who believe in freedom defy
The acts of violence among us,
And instead create peace with justice.
Freedom provides a wholesome life together,
Revealing everybody's shadow is the same color.

Tear down the walls of injustices and
Lift up the will of hope for the hopeless,
Let all hear our peaceful cries.
Hope is the desire made to fulfill one another,
Accepting everybody's shadow is the same color.

Do not seek revenge against the avengers,
But strain to teach the world the opposite.
A creator defies revenge, death, and horrors,
Looking for a commandment fit for a lover,
Believing everybody's shadow is the same color.

A creator has given the world the same universe,
The moon and the stars decorate the skies
And the sun shines equally on all the creatures,
Calling upon the nature of life a father and a mother,
Acknowledging everybody's shadow is the same color.

John H. Green
St. Augustine, FL

Chigger

An invisible, odorless, tasteless
time-bomb of touch.
Silent but deadly.

A gentle jeweler
stringing bracelets of red beads
that cost plenty of scratch.

A timorous, time-release
commie-colored capsule
itching to feast on fisher-persons.

Smaller than a bread crumb.

The Adolf Eichmann of sleep.

Claude Lee
Topeka, KS

A Cowboy's Tale

The cowboy was old, he wouldn't last long,
He'd rode his last bull, played his last song.
His hands were all gnarled and broken from work,
But that's not important where memories lurk.
He sat on the porch, the memories were clear,
He could remember the season, the year.
It was down in the season, late in the fall.
If you listen real close you could hear winter call.
Riding the grub-line, working for keep,
Two square meals and a warm place to sleep.
He was down in the barn feeding the cattle
When a pretty young miss wanted her saddle.
She smiled very softly, he nodded his head;
She turned bright crimson, his thoughts she had read.
All winter long they met in the barn,
They'd ride in the meadow, he'd tell her tall yarns.
When spring came again, their feelings ran deep,
But he had an itch that just wouldn't keep.
He woke one morning far from the ranch
Knowing full well there was no second chance.
He spent many years running away,
Wishing and praying that he would have stayed.
Now he sits on the porch and rocks to and fro,
Dreaming his dreams til his time to go.

Paul L. Petitt
Gillette, WY

A Daughter's Heart

My heart yearns for my father at my door.
My heart yearns to see him once more.

My heart yearns for his never ending love.
My heart yearns for him to swoop in like a dove.

My heart yearns to feel his special hugs.
My heart yearns for him to quit the drugs.

My heart yearns for his sins to be forgiven.
My heart yearns for the life he should be living.

My heart yearns to see his manly face.
My heart yearns for him to be blessed by grace.

My heart mourns for my father taken from the door.
My heart mourns for me not seeing him anymore.

My heart mourns for me not hearing what it is he loves.
My heart mourns for not seeing him fly up above.

My heart mourns for the jailing of his hugs.
My heart mourns because he hasn't quit the drugs.

My heart mourns for me not knowing if he's forgiven.
My heart mourns for me not helping him do his living.

My heart mourns for me not touching his tender face.
My heart mourns for his decisions made against grace.

This poem is true, I mourn and yearn.
But it is my father who should get your concern.

He needs your prayers, I won't give up
Because I know he can be an amazing grown-up.

Jessica Burchfield
White Pine, TN

My poem is about me and my dad. He has made some pretty stupid choices, but he is still an amazing father. I don't write poems often, but when I do, they are mostly about my dad. My mom, brothers, and stepdad support me fully. I love them very much.

Once There Were Nine

Once upon a time, there was a family of nine:
Ma and Pa, and seven of awe.
Ma was Tunney, no one knows why.
Pop, Joe Sr., you'll learn by and by.
Big brother was Joe Jr. , they called him JoJo.
Paul was to follow, and they all said, "Oh no!"
Next there was Jean, golden-haired and lean.
Then came Judy, like a pirate with his booty.
Along came Eddie, a little late but ready,
Kept from golf by the whooping cough.
Then it was Rita, the sixth to pop,
As Tunney exclaimed, "Please Lord, make it stop!"
Lo and behold came the last little tyke,
So cute and so smart, his name shall be Mike!

Joseph J. Ulliman
Moscow, ID

A few years ago, I started to write a quick ditty about my family, my father, mother and six siblings. At that time, I wrote about my parents, who are deceased, and myself. Then I thought, not claiming to be a great poet, it would be interesting to have each sibling write their own ditty. Most recently I sent them an email and this is what I got back, a jingle from each. I am the oldest and they are, in order to the youngest, seventy-eight to sixty-five. A thought for other families.

My Perfect Mother

My mommy told me about a poetry contest
Asked me to write one, thinking I'm the best
I've always been happy to be her son
It would make her so proud if I won
She is a Christian, the sweetest in the world
I sure love my mommy, the perfect little girl
She's always stood by me, through thick and thin
Even when I'm bad, even when I sin
My dad is so lucky to find such a girl
Never raised her voice, most perfect in this world
She loves everyone no matter their race
Seeing the love all over her face
I wish the whole world had a mother like me
We'd all come together, and then we'd all see
That love is the answer to everything
Heaven awaiting with love it will bring
Thank you, dear Jesus, for being so bold
Even through persecution, love's all that you told
One day we'll be together in Heaven again
Being with loved ones and all our friends
Death isn't real, it's all in our minds
And when we get there, everyone's kind
I could write all day about this eternal love
'Cause there's no end to poetry when it comes from above
Thank you, Lord, for being so kind
'Cause all of this poetry came from your mind

Rob Smith
Sperryville, VA

The Shore

Life here is washed meticulously by the waves.
　　Life here is dampened by salty sprays.
Shorelines are usually boundaries of sand.
　　Shorelines are the places that touch all lands.
Plants here are tested by harshness and gentle breeze.
　　Plants here are planted here by the sandy squeeze.
Gulls are a sign that all the world was made to be free.
　　Gulls are a reminder that there is a shore to the sea.

Jim Heisler
Milwaukee, WI

The Sea

　　The sea goes in, the sea goes out
　　The never-ending sea
　　It never stops for anyone
　　The never-ending sea
　　It comes, it goes, it never stops
　　The never-ending sea
　　The sea comes in and brings its treasure
　　And always takes it back
　　It never likes to part with them
　　It never stays for anyone
　　The never-ending sea

Patricia Retter
Vandergrift, PA

Beware

Beware of demons, as they're all around,
You're quite lost and wanna be found.
God is truth and will light your way:
Just knock
Kneel down
Pray

He knows our hearts and what's on our minds,
He'll ne'er forsake you,
He'll make the time.
He doesn't like ugly and beauty's skin deep.
Life's what you make it;
Just remember
There are penalties to reap.

So parents, teach your children;
Ignorance—no excuse!
God, our heavenly Father, watches o'er us and speaks
Through His word—truth!

Lynn Laningham
San Antonio, TX

Lynn Laningham resides in San Antonio, TX, and has been blessed by God, family, and friends. I wrote about life's events, spiritual beliefs, and encouragement and support of others. My children are grown with families of their own. My selection, "Beware," was penned while attending church services. The sermon inspired "Beware"—life inspires my writing as well as the beauty which surrounds me.

A Tribute to My Father on Father's Day

Can I ever forget your genuine words of truthfulness
That lifted my spirit with deep content?
Those very pleasant moments of happiness at its best
That can never be erased but stands out amongst all the tests,
Your kindness makes me all inclined to boast
Of that special person who did the journey all in full,
And always tried to make it good,
You stayed and never walked away.
Accepting the challenges that came your way,
For this child you saw so dear,
Who needed strength along the way
I lift my head up high and thank you more as days go by.

The sheep that graze in the meadow
Would think of you as the greatest fellow,
You are that one who is always there
For all of us who need your care.
You have always been of reassurance
To those of us who needed comfort,
In my opinion you have passed the test
Of being a father above the rest.

The stars in the Heavens would reiterate
Those sentimental words I reinstate
That filled my world with so much laughter,
Not only now but forever after.

Those solemn words of—I love you!

Marelina James
West Haverstraw, NY

Starting the Day Off Right

Sizzle as it lies, hot
Sweat brims as the core lights
Heat growing, as the dark bottom warms
Reach under
Flip around
Again heat, sweat
My lips quiver
Anxious for it, yes
Body needy, gotta have it
Give me
Finally, just right
Pull in my mouth
Delicious
Syrupy drizzle sliding off surface
Morning
Perfect pancakes

Anjili Jani
Cortlandt Manor, NY

A Fairy's Love Potion

"This is fabulous, this is great
What an exciting Love Potion I can create!"
Said the fairy's assistant
His eyes gleaming with desire and persistence
Laid his hands on a colorless glass flask
Began pouring red, white and blue
In a vivid spectrum of the rainbow's hue,
Purple, green, pink and yellow
Fanciful, fantastic, flamboyant fellow
Just then, Florence the fairy flew in
"Fred, young lad
Rabbit's foot and four-leaf clover you must add
A dash of lavender in half an hour
Hurry, there is no time to waste
Time is of the essence and this should not be late"
Attracting a fairy can be fruitful for you
When you believe in them your dreams do come true
A puff of smoke emanates high up in the air
Just then, Fred giggled to declare
"Here in this bottle is fulfillment and love for two
You be the judge of what to do
As we sincerely hope it works for you"

Savitrie Sally Elliott
Flushing, NY

Be True to Yourself

May you see the truth in all you see
May your heart be happy, and your will be free
Be forever grateful for that first sunrise
The first light of day that ever touched your eyes
And all the days since, and you will find that you're wise
Accept all that greets you in each coming year
You will find that you're stronger
Than if you lived in fear
Everyone struggles and has their bad times
But you must not let that stop you
For your soul was made to fly
If you do the best you can in all that you do,
You will see all weakness vanish
And the life you live is true

Barbara McKenna *"ANGELA"*
Lockport, NY

Enhancing the Present

How do I heighten or intensify historic buildings, which now lie in disrepair all over our land?

Is there any way by my hand, whether old and wrinkled or smooth and suntanned, to improve their already-quality, still good?

What about that one that once stately stood down that rugged countryside road where the famous patriot long ago abode?

Is there not something I can do to raise funds, their preservation to pursue?

Of course, I can if I will expand my efforts to get more to join the band of legacy-minded people over the land whose interest is to seriously elevate these various buildings to their original state.

Modern day hopefuls will be my bequest, ones I can interest I will definitely behest.

After all, it could be a part of their own birthright that will soon become a more welcomed sight when the decaying columns we reinforce and strengthen pillars long of course.

Everyone will be so intensely proud as we definitely lift the cloud of what once was a sad part of the past and seek to develop a design that will last.

Images now will be maximized as the present with the past is realized.

When on these historic buildings we now gaze, our heritage is expressed for many—
always!

Bobbie J. Burnett
Russellville, KY

A Divine Deception

Ephemerellas drifting by
Knot the tippet to a fly

Struggling mayfly, trouts' repast
Arching rod-tip, looping cast

Touching down in eddy's ripple
Tempting trout who dare to dimple

Carried by the current's drift
A splashing rise, and rod-tip lift

Betrayed by feathers lashed to hook
Wildly leaping, fly-line shook

Noble adversaries met
Pink-striped sides caressed by net

Fly removed from gasping lip
Returned to stream from angler's grip

William J. Earley
Farmington, NM

The Nostalgic Indian Friend

The dreams of an insomniac, who is also just alive,
toss and turn, the insomniacal-mood
as though, the memories
are spasmodic,
when it truly is the lower-back-re-injury,
that defies the story, the 36-hour day of *The 36-hour Day*
and the worrisome
state of realization
is waking
and the way of the
insomniacal-mood that,
defied the half-filled glass of sweet wine,
that soothed the insomniacal-mood, to sleep
is old already,
Much like the days of old,
when I was young.
I was old!
And, the way of life.

Sherry R. Neeley
Thomasville, NC

I am a person who is handicapped. I discovered the joy of writing; I struggled through my own emotional battles within my heart and from, of course, those I met along the way of my own life. But I must admit that I had to come out of my own emotional depression, and writing became a very practical part of that. I've been through a difficult time of change that is totally of my own traditional upbringing and, of course, my own will power to change. I enjoy writing for my own well-being. I am a Christian. I enjoy being my own boss!

Look Around

Look around and
you will see
what God created
for you and me.
A sky as far as the
eye can see,
majestic mountains
with rippling streams.
Oh, so peaceful, oh
so serene.
Look around and
you will see
what God created:
you and me.

Donna M. O'Neill
New Hope, MN

Happy Birthday

When you wake up and see the sun,
You'll be so happy your day has begun.
This is your very special day—
My wishes to you, I want to say:
From every hour and each minute,
Your heart be filled with happiness in it.
For all your days and nights come through,
May all your dreams come true for you.

Patricia Sicurelli
Seaford, NY

Untitled

Horses are sweet
horses are kind.
Horses can gallop
high or low.
Horses can
run fast. Horses
can run slow.
But what
matters the most
is your love
for the horse!

Jada Bennett
Philadelphia, PA

Something to Think About

Imagine—if you will,
A grove of redwood trees
Being buffeted by
A very blustery breeze.

Visualize just one
Virtually crashing down,
with a high wailing cry
and loud thunderous sound.

Imagine—if you can,
What damage has been done,
to all it did besiege,
extend and overrun.

You can't, you say! For you
Have never been one to confound.
It's what a soldier feels
As friends are laid to ground.

Through reflections echoed,
Seedlings projected strong.
Nary shall rise again—
Bereft of vestige gone.

Gary W. Enos
Hayward, CA

Why!

The bell rang and I hurried to my seat,
a strange woman walked in
who I didn't really want to meet.
She introduced herself as Ms. Kim.

She wore glasses and braces,
she looked like a real nerd.
She set down a picture frame with recognizable faces,
in their hands were some red roses and a fake bird.

She wore long purple pants,
with little black heels,
even wore a tie that had little red ants.
She had on a sticker that said "save the seals."

I can't believe I have to go the whole school year
with this teacher who will only eat a club
when I could have been on field trips to the pier.
When she was done she said, "And I'll be your Sub."

Jamie Patton
Highland, CA

Dear Mom and Dad

I'm in a special place right now,
The place we here call home.
And since I know you miss me,
From Heaven I send this poem.

It was rainy when I left that day,
But I'm where it's clear and bright.
I don't feel pain or sadness here,
But I'll dream of you at night.

Thanks for sticking by my side
Each day to wish me well.
I want you to know that I'm okay,
And I love you more than words can tell.

So when you see a deer I'd prize
Or a fish waiting to bite,
Think of them as signs from me,
For these things brought me much delight.

Send my love to sis Raelynn
And baby Jayden Ray.
Train them in the ways of God,
And when they are old they will not stray.

You needn't worry anymore;
God has me in His care.
Look around, and you will find
In all things beautiful, I'm everywhere.

Ronell J. Smith
Mt Pleasant, PA

I did not personally know Brandon; my aunt is a friend of his family. Brandon was fourteen years old and passed away October 27, 2011. In June, 2011 he suffered severe chemical burns to his lungs as a result of smoking synthetic marijuana from a Pez candy dispenser. A double lung transplant in late September was unsuccessful. It was an honor for me to write this poem and be asked to read it at Brandon's funeral. I pray that you are as touched by Brandon's poem as the hundreds of people who passed through the funeral home that early November day.

The Caregiver

Roses are red
Violets are blue,
I'd known Sandy Learn
Over two months now.

And she's too cool to be true!
She's a caregiver for
Bill and Shirley McNeece,

She keeps them in line. . .
If she doesn't they
will fall on their behind. . .

Julie Rounsfull
Port Angeles, WA

It's Never Too Late

Every time you try to do your best. . someone tries to prove you wrong.
Just remember it's just a test, and deep inside you must stay strong.
It's never too late. . for what you want never give up what you want in
your life.
Continue to dream the impossible dream. . and one day you will see
the light.
There are days when you want to cry, when you're feeling down and
alone.
You just want someone by your side, someone there to call your own.
Never too late for what you want. . let nobody take that away. . .
Tell yourself that you still know, "It's never too late."
Never too late to make a wish. It's never too late to reach for your goals.
It's never too late to make a promise to yourself, there is always hope for
tomorrow.

Cynthia Winkfield
Columbus, OH

Peopling Lures

Is this feeling rapture or rupture?
The result of a mystical big pin? Or a head doctor cure?
Is this sensation some medicinal fix?
Or is it what comes upon latching hold of one's lure?
I don't know!

I'm naught but a being swimming in this molecule mix
Seeing to see, feeling to feel, wanting to miss no trick,
Trying to burst through this physical deal—lured.
Oh, push, poke, and pursue experiments and kicks—

Beyond, above, a different air, that's the cure
I seek. And it's not obscure
At all! Rapture's ruptures come to those doers
Who are yanked out—pulled by invisible (internal) lures.

But is the feeling rapture or rupture?

Doug Talbert
Catale Rock, CO

*Cheerful. Intense. Intelligent. Driven. Contentious. Humorous. Easy-going.
Life-long learner. A seventeen-year alternative high school teacher. . .
convincing hard-core non-learners to adopt curiosity about living. Enigmatic
inspirations—"Come, Ariel"—what inspired this poem? Watching dolphins
taking above water air and diving back down into their lives.*

My Shadow

I have lost all sanity
My heart grows heavy and weak
No faith have I in humanity
Peace within still I seek

I have fallen into the dark
My delicate wings have broken
I never got to make my mark
At least now I have spoken

Lying at the bottom, alone
Slowly dying where shadows are kept
Where the light has never shone
Buried alive in my despair, I wept

Kristen Hildebrandt
Franklin, TX

I Don't Know

I don't know how it started
I don't know how it will end
But all I know, today you are
My very special friend.

I don't know when it started
I really do not care
I am just so glad to have a friend
So sweet, so kind, so rare.

I don't know what of tomorrow—
If it will bring us joy or sorrow—
But whatever comes I know it will
Bring us closer together still.

I don't know what would happen
If we had never met,
I'm pretty sure I'd rather have you
Than a kitten as a pet.

I don't know any other
Who is quite the same as you,
You stick closer than a brother,
Yes, that's what you always do.

I do know that I love you,
I do know that I care,
I do know that our friendship
Will last throughout the years.

Cathy Anderson-Frost
Brooklyn, NY

Daughter of Mine

Another sunrise brings a child
Never to regret
Never to walk away
In God's blessing, I am touched
Ever loving all who love her
Like a breeze, intangible,
Lovable, loving child of mine
Even to be my daughter,
To be loved by her, is a delight

Cheryl Mallow
Watertown, WI

Untitled

Voices, voices in my head
screaming, tearing at my skull
trying to get out
my skull is splitting open
I feel no pain

Carrie Hamby
Bartlett, TN

I am thirty-two years old and the youngest of three children. I was sick a lot when I was younger, in and out of hospitals a lot. Both the doctors and my parents thought I would not learn how to walk. I did, but not until I was two. I was born with one side of my chest caved in; I had that repaired when I was nine.

A Hundred Little Cedar Trees

A hundred little cedar trees
Ladybugs on the fence
A trail goes to a waterfall
And views that are immense

A creek flows by the driveway
And winds on down the hill
Many places to park a chair
To enjoy the rocks and rills

Elderberries lined the land
And gave you lots of jelly
The bear came to pay a visit
And fill his great big belly

The woodpile says winter will come
With snow and wind and sleet
The wood all cut and stacked up high
Will warm your hands and feet

Four balconies where you can sit
Amid the cedar smell
For reading, scheming and dreaming
While the woods cast their spell

The shed was home to many a pet:
Cats, dogs and who knows what
They worked their way into the house
More loving than their hut

Marion Elkerton
North Hollywood, CA

When I Die

When I die,
I don't want my family looking in my casket,
Laughing and shedding their tears.
As a puppy abused day by day
Not knowing when its next meal is going to be,
Chained to a pole all beaten and bruised
So his master could have his way.
He breaks the chain loose and he runs away,
Never looking back at the master who had his way.
Alone they say I shall die, for I closed the doors to my past life
And the master shall never again have his way.
When I die, I want my husband here;
He showed me he cares,
He taught me how to hug and all about love.
He gave me his heart
And for that we shall never part.
Alone they say I shall die,
Alone not am I, when I die.
I want the angels from Heaven above
To surround my casket so I can feel their everlasting love
And the Lord to send an angel
To show the world that I died with love.

Lupe Jennings
Amarillo, TX

Little Girl Lost

A butterfly fell,
I saw it today.
What had happened
that made air go away?
A flower's head,
it fell to the ground.
What had happened?
What was that sound?
I heard it today,
I didn't understand,
angels were weeping
all over the land.
A moment so brief,
you'll hold her so dear
forever in your heart
as she was here.
She is not with us,
she floats up above
watching from Heaven
with her Grandmother's love.

Michele Rutherford
Dublin, PA

My Aunt Gina and Uncle Paul were looking forward to the birth of their daughter. Tragically, Heather died just shortly after her birth. We were all looking forward to meeting her and, sadly, all we got was to mourn for her. Tragedy can tear a family apart, but this has only made them stronger as individuals and as a couple. Heather is just waiting for them in Heaven, where they will meet again someday. They are my family—I am lucky to call them mine—and we all love them very much.

The Calling

God calls us from all nations
  and welcomes us into His fold.
The Holy Spirit empowers us
  to do as we've been told.

It matters not to Jesus
  the color of our face—
Black, white, red or yellow—
  we all can receive His grace.

Why should anyone live in poverty—
  no place to lay his head—
No food, no job, no hope for the day—
  bowed by earth's burdens instead?

We're in this world to do the job
  given by our Lord in love—
To reach out to each other
  and share God's gifts from above.

So, avoid the road that leads to
  everlasting misery.
Just pick up your cross and follow
  God's call to eternity.

Anna L. Shelton
Washington, DC

My Virginia

My life's journeys took me far up north to Wisconsin.
I stood beside Lake Superior's celestial shores.
I looked out across the shining, deep sea waters
where ships sailed from distant shores.
I walked along the sand dunes
where the Indians used to roam.
The arms of old Virginia always welcome me home.
I traveled through North Carolina.
I visited Kentucky and Tennessee.
I gazed up at lofty mountain peaks,
watched the sun sink into the sea.
I am proud to be from Virginia
with her mountains that reach toward the sky,
the ocean breezes where seagulls fly,
the stately homes where presidents
and great statesmen were born,
with numerous battlefields where brave soldiers died,
weary and worn.
Among the flower-decked fields and woodland glens,
Virginia holds the secrets of a child therein.
And over the earth many miles I may roam,
the arms of old Virginia always welcome me home.

Josephine Stidham
Petersburg, VA

*I am a native Virginian. I was born October 23, 1930 in Goochland County,
VA. I attended Sande Hook Elementary School and graduated from
Goochland High School in 1950. It was my tenth grade English teacher,
who was witty and fun-loving, that brought poetry alive for me. Later I
married and became the mother of eight wonderful children which I raised
alone with the Lord's help. Now it's my time to see if my talent for writing
poetry holds any reward or recognition for me.*

Stars!

Not every star has a spark
Like the ones you see at dark
As you gaze towards the sky
On a bench in some lonesome park
Yet something out of reach
Is the thing you'd like to keep
And that is why you weep
But don't you cry
Dry your eyes
For a star to you I bring
It's a starfish
On a string!
May you smile always :)

Dakota L. Luce
Tomahawk, WI

Don't Cry for Me. . .

Don't cry for me when I'm gone.
Don't cry for me walking home.
Don't wish how you could've
Made things better.
Don't say my name as if you're proud.
Don't sing songs of sorrow, don't
Dream of what could have been me.
Don't cry for me when I'm gone.
Don't share your thoughts of me,
Don't even dream of me in your sleep.
Don't look, don't touch old pictures and clothes.
Don't mourn for me when I'm gone.
Don't come to see me in my grave.
Your time has passed, that moment
Did not last. So don't blame me for
My death, blame yourself.
The lack of love and affection, attention
And conversation, is what you failed.
So don't grieve for me when I'm
Gone. Don't celebrate, don't drink or
smoke. Just light a white candle,
But don't weep for me when I'm gone.

Sim-ia "Poet" Johnson
Brooklyn, NY

I have come a long way from the streets of East New York, Brooklyn, and at twenty-seven years old, it's safe to say those same streets made me who I am today. With my mother's ambition in my strut, I strive to be the best I am set out to be. Therefore, it pours out in my verses. For instance, the inspiration behind "Don't Cry For Me" stemmed from the resentment I had towards my father, the overall hatred I had toward those who judged me upon my coming out with my sexuality, and the strength of my spirituality. When I go into "my place," "my zone," I give it all I've got! I like to call it "raw poetry" because I touch all bases. "Don't Cry For Me" is for that young teenager crying for attention before he/she commits suicide, or that young adult seeking spiritual refuge or how about the middle-aged woman who was raped and is constantly reminded when she looks into the eyes of her offspring. . . I believe this is just the beginning for me. So I invite you to "get to know me."

Portrait of a Glut

Vats of lard melting, sliming down
through and through the arteries—
not a picturesque image

Sodium pellets encrust this portrait of disgust
with deep fat splatters
upon the hemisphere of sensible choices

As the fat immerses and saturates
your taste buds blossom
to degrees of disagreement

You devour more salt as you lick your deranged wounds—
you plunge ever forward
into what you consume

As I draw pesticides, formaldehyde
and other ancillary chemicals
incessantly into my vital organs

We both surreptitiously paint over our same old muddy palates
always discouraged in our weakness,
conscious only of an unchangeable horizon

I brazen out of turn my dismay for your dreadful canvas—
you say it's not for me to pipe up
and assert anything candid

You resound from beneath your bubble-like armor
reacting to how I articulate myself—
do as I say, not as I do. I retort, "Touché."

Janene Prenzno
Mesa, AZ

Birthday Poem

Here it is, another year
And I didn't forget to send you some cheer;
I hope you plan to celebrate
And maybe someone will bake you a cake.

I bet you thought I'd forget—
If I had. . I. would have regret
Giving you this birthday rhyme
And I'm so glad I thought of you in time.

Go have a fun-filled day
'Cause it's the best way
To laugh and to smile
And that will feel good for a while.

I'm sending this message your way
To have a sensational day,
Celebrate with a party today
'Cause it's your special day.

Don't forget for heaven's sake
To blow all the candles out on your cake,
And I hope your wish comes true
For a very special person like you.

Here's to hoping next year
I'll remember to send you some cheer
So you can be surprised
And put some sparkle in your eyes.

Let's have ice cream. . let's have cake,
Let's celebrate for goodness sake!

Cindy Watkins Ledford
Homer, GA

Time

I think about the time when I was young
The days were long and full of fun
We used to play all made-up games
We even sometimes changed our names
I dressed up in my mother's clothes
And fixed my hair with pretty bows
I thought about my years to come
And all about my dreams and fears
It sometimes brings my eyes to tears
Hoping I made all the right choices
I started to hear those little voices
They told me there was more to come
That for me my life had just begun
I met a boy who caught my eye
It seemed to be a dream come true
And we married to my delight the man
was just so very right
We lived a life full of joy; first a girl then boy
Time has passed and family grew
With grandchildren making my dreams come true
I still think about when I was young
When days were long and full of fun

Rita J. DiTillo
Waterbury, CT

I wrote this poem while my husband was dying of Alzheimer's. It sort of sums up my life and joining his life. He died 10-2-13.

Immortal

Underneath the dark lashes are emerald eyes
The beautiful creature's face framed with dark curly lies
Red lips and pink cheeks cannot hide her wicked grin
Or the depravity of her sin
Her heart is as cold as ice
And as dangerous as her fangs that absorb her host's life
Her voice when she laughs is like a devil's siren
Leading you inside a wolf's den
Her skin shines pale in the moonlight
Making her the embodiment of death in the night
Her black dress flutters in the wind sounding like a raven's wing
As her lips sing
I gravitate toward her as a star is pulled inside a black hole
My doomed soul
My death was near
As she got closer I was sure she could smell my fear
A scream rose inside my throat
But it was stopped by her hand upon my coat
She brushed it aside exposing my collar
Licking her lips, she began to lean down farther
A prick of pain
And the next thing I heard was the sound of beautiful rain
I opened my eyes to her face
Her expression filled with a type of dark grace
In that moment, I knew I was immortal
There was something worse than death, more fatal

Kayla Daley
Hattiesburg, MS

A Great Man

A man of strength, a man of right,
A man who always had to fight

John Fitzgerald Kennedy was this man
Who fought and fought to save this land

Two years, ten months and two days in office
He seldom took a drink of coffee

John Fitzgerald Kennedy was this man
Who fought and fought to save this land

On this cold and cloudy day, riding through Dallas to make a speech
Little did he know this was his last time to the people he would reach

John Fitzgerald Kennedy was this man
Who fought and fought to save this land

On November twenty-second, nineteen sixty-three,
An assassin's bullet struck him in the head,
Oh no, no, no, this great man was dead

John Fitzgerald Kennedy was this man
Who fought and fought to save this land

Freddie Mae McGee
Bossier City, LA

Secrets

If you had a secret that's killing you
And you had to tell your new friend,
You were scared to tell, but just had
to,
Not knowing how bad it will end—
When you tell your friend it is then
out.
Once they know, you can't take it
back,
You will want to scream out loud and
shout,
Everything you see, you will want to
smack,
You will loose strength every day and
have regret,
You will want to leave this place and
go,
Something inside you won't let you
leave just yet,
They beg you to stay, you cry and
say no

Maria Pia Collell
Mission Viejo, CA

The Mind Is Free

You tell me of a place where souls can interweave
And that your heart can see it from below
Amid the foggy river mist.

You claim it's there and say I must agree.
It blossoms past the water dark
A place where love is just
In ageless peace—

In which the mind is free.
You step ahead
And call
Me
But all
I feel is dread;
This world I cannot see.

You say release
All of the things I trust
And then with ease I can embark.
You fail to understand this cannot be.

You scold me, thinking I resist,
Yet you ignore what little that I know:
How can a man accept what he cannot believe?

Martin Groff
Lebanon, PA

A Salute to Stress

Stress, the result of a state of mind
Born from the ingrained need
To please others,
Rather than myself;

Stress, the cause of stomach knots,
Heart palpitations, and headaches,
Even a backache,
And always sweaty palms;

Stress, the hand that pushes me
To always be on time,
To do more than my best,
To be very accurate;

Stress, to you I say, "Stop!"
No longer will I let you rule me;
No longer will I listen
To your destructive ways;

I have replaced you, Stress,
With another, better lover
Who helps me shut out the demands
And offers me the gift of amazing peace.

Stand with me, strength of all creation;
Together we will shove aside
The busyness of this harried life,
And stroll outside to view the stars.

Sally D. Brown
Glastonburg, CT

Sally D. Brown is a former English teacher, tutor, preschool teacher, church administrator, and ordained minister in the United Church of Christ. Presently she enjoys writing, reading, traveling with her husband, participating in book and discussion groups, and being with her children and four grandchildren. Sally earned her BA at the University of Maine in Orono, her MA in education at the University of St. Joseph, and her MDiv at Yale Divinity School. A lifelong learner and writer, she enjoys sharing her feelings and observations through poetry. The pressure she felt within and in people around her inspired this poem.

Something for Someone

I have something for someone
It's been remade like new
Out of broken boards and timbers
But I am sure it will please you

With the help of my friend
All the pieces we did find
Then rebuilt the broken structure
Now it is one of a kind

Although I have completed building
And the hardest part is done
I must continue working
Because improvements have begun

There must always be improvements
Because you deserve the best
And through all the storms in life
It will always stand the test

Now before you get your gift
There is something you must see
You must share my love today
Because the gift to you—is me

Robert Nelson
Sherbrooke, QC

To My Angel on Christmas Day

Christmas Day is here again, my love, crisp as the morning dew,
And for the last twenty-five years it has been my honor to spend it with you.
  I look in your eyes and see all the love just as it was all those years ago,
And when you look in my eyes I hope you see a love that will never let go.
  When I look at you I see the woman of my desire,
That when I get close to you I am filled with a fire.
  I want to make a place where you and I can be together
Filled with life, joy, happiness, laughter and love forever.
  I want to see your eyes sparkle like they did way back when,
When life was fun, I want to see you happy again.
  I want music and dancing and joy in our life,
I need you to know how very special it is to me that you are my wife.
  You are the one I need to make happy, the one I need to please,
For you see, my love, it is for you and you alone that I will get down on my knees.
  I will always hold you on a pedestal, my love,
So that you can look down at the world from above.
  So all the beauty and good things are there for you to see,
That there neither is nor never was anyone but you for me.
  You and I have grown so much together and in so many ways in this time,
You are still the love of my life, my beautiful wife, and I am so glad you're mine.

Daniel Norris
Tulsa, OK

One Little Thing

So sorry this is late,
but I needed time to think,
to make this poem special,
I needed one little thing,
the phrase that means the most,
above all,
so late or not,
here it comes,
the one little thing I've been waiting on,
    "I love you so much Daddy,
     thanks for everything!"

There I said it,
the one little thing,
and I'll say it again
because that's it,
the one thing,
the special thing,
the most important thing anyone could possibly say
to a guy so special,
to a guy so close to my heart,
    "I love you so much Daddy,
     thanks for everything!"

Kirstin Walz
Elkton, MD

Untitled

I was partially raised on popcorn
And soft drinks.
"Popcorn in a bucket of water will float," once said by a white foreman,
Among other jobs nearby, people, where self went to earn money and
less boredom.
Anyway, could this be a side dish?
Getting to something that's not tasty,
A white man with spouse, chum, or friend got so comfortable,
He returned to get his wallet tucked between the wall and seat.
Being unsure as to whether this group had, at least one, child tagging
along.

Jasper Sessoms
Tarboro, NC

Insomnia

The best and most accurate description
of my long sleepless nights
it may be by invoking my sauntering
in a suspension-state

Wherein I can't do anything
but to remember repeatedly
all those events occurred
along the times we spent together,
neatly displayed in front of my eyes
in a fragmentary and recurrent form,
not evoked by the memory,
but in an arbitrary and spontaneous way,
like impelled by eagerness
to preserve its own validity,
stubbornly attached as living experiences,
not mere memories

They come up facing upon me
with strong obstinacy
withholding entirely their own shade,
its warmth . . its fragrance. . .

Tactile sensations that flood not only my mind,
but all over inside me

Hector Vargas
Phoenix, AZ

My Lady

The most wonderful lady that I ever knew
Is with Jesus in Heaven, but she is here with us, too
Her address has changed, yes, that's very true,
But my heart is longing to be with her, too.
I loved her so dearly that lady of mine.
She was so precious, her smile was divine,
But the best thing about her was she was all mine.
A lady, a Christian, a beauty 'twas true,
And truly not many would compare with her, too.
The mother of my children, the pride of my life,
None other than my dear loving wife.

Dennis L. Payne
Murfreesboro, IN

In August of 1980 our family was in a very serious auto accident. We were hit by someone just under the legal limit then. My daughter and I weren't expected to live. Our four-year-old son had both legs broken. Our daughter actually expired, but was revived. My wife (and children's mother) was killed.

Will You?

Will you love me after tomorrow?
Will you love me when we are gone?
Will you take the time to stop and cry
Will you leave flowers? I know life goes on
Will you sit by your father and mother
Will you give us a minute to share
Will you ask so many questions why?
Will you find peace of mind
Will you find laughter or a smile
Will you look down on both of us
We did the best we could
Will you let the good outweigh the bad
Will memories try to destroy all the love
We gave to you, all we had?
Will you love us when you cry
Time goes on will you love us or will you let it go?
Will you remember all the time we had in our life?
Will you remember it was for all you girls in our life?
Time has a way and life goes on just remember today—if we come
back to all of you will you want us to stay

Carolyn Shallenberger
Hamilton, IL

Untitled

Oh Mother, our mother
Sweet angel divine
You were one classy lady
Throughout your long life

When we were all children
Still under your wing
You loved us and taught us
Life's most basic things

Whereever you went
Perfect strangers would stare
Then walk up to tell you
How beautiful you are

Your singing and dancing
Still ring in our ears
And we all feel so blessed
For your eighty-nine years

Now dance up to Heaven
Where your family awaits
With their arms outstretched to you
At Heaven's gate

Then smile down upon us
With that special sweet grin
For one of these days
We will see you again

Angie Pettigrew
DeLand, FL

A Get Well Wish

From your sister's sister-in-law

When things get tough
as they often do
it's hard to find a window
to look through

We tend to struggle
we twist and turn
like a leaf in the wind
as if there was nothing to learn

Then a light shines on
there is a glow
the feel of a warm thought
a blessed hello

A kind word drifts in
a smile that shows care
a basket of flowers
a sweet smell of fresh air

It's a tiny bit easier
to lay down one's head
to think of the good stuff
and all that was said

Hope is a reason
love says it best
we must march to the battle
and then we can rest

Ruth Heller
Glastonbury, CT

My poems just come to me. It could be midnight or six a.m.. I've been writing all my adult life. My poems are long and short, funny and foolish depending on my life at the moment. I've sent poems to family members and friends on occasion. Once in a while I've been told the poem had meant a great deal. It's my secret life. It's just plain fun.

Lions at the Gate

My dogs and I, we like to play,
unfortunately no play today.
The grass, the trees are pavement, glass,
we dream at night of days gone past.
A little room is where we dwell,
a room close to the gates of hell.
For when we walk, I hold them near
for there is much that I could fear.
Strangers lay upon the living room floor,
you never know who will enter the door.
Young girls cry out in despair,
their mothers on drugs, don't care, don't care.
The bathroom is where they like to slam
their drug of choice, they're damned, they're damned.
The house gets loud and dirty too,
people are sick, but not the flu.
The plumbing's broke and fridge is bare,
their next high is all they care.
The bedbugs, roaches never rest,
tucked in the couches in their nests.
They pass the pipe and smoke all night,
laugh, talk, they argue beyond daylight.
They smile, they steal from one another,
friend or foe or even mother.
And as we walk, I watch our steps,
a needle once in someone's neck.
A little room is where we dwell,
a room close to the gates of hell.
My dogs and I, we like to play,
unfortunately no play today.
My dogs are lions at that gate,
protecting me from dark fate.
My room a sanctuary aglow.
For God lives here, I know, I know.

Bonne Cavana
Sun City, AZ

My Friend Lonely

One dreary day while walking alone
Humming the tune to some old sad song
Longing for a friend to confide
Someone to walk close by my side
I heard a voice on the cold north wind
Softly it said, *I will be your friend*
What is your name, if I might ask?
I don't need you if it will not last
I am called Lonely and many know me well
Whether it will last, only time will tell
Come along then, my unseen friend
Perhaps you can help this old heart to mend
I thought this might last only a day
But we had so much in common, he decided to stay
Lonely quickly became my closest friend
The one on whom I could always depend
Even in a crowd he was always there
Ready and willing my troubles to share
Oh! We shared a few laughs over the years
But mostly we just shared the tears
I continue on with Lonely at my side
While my life ebbs as the tide
I have a few more promises to keep
Then Lonely and I together will sleep the dreamless sleep

Bob N. White
Russellville, AR

Sitting Vigil

Alone in her room
in a deep sleep
she is slipping away.
Outside it is springtime—
life starts anew—
here it is coming to an end.
On her wall, cards and pictures,
smiling babies,
the beginning, then the end.
On the street the bustling traffic—
nurses, aids out in the hall—
life goes on.
I want to hold her,
cradle, shelter,
pave the way, to this other world.

Katharina K. Martin
Danvers, MA

*My writing is very plain and simple. I truly am flattered, but also feel good that
my poem received recognition. I started to write things down later in my life,
now I am over seventy years of age. As I go about my day, daydreaming, my
thoughts take on a poetic form. "Sitting Vigil" is dear to me, close to my heart
as I am a volunteer for Hospice of the North Shore and Greater Boston.*

If I Were

If I were ice and you were fire
Would you melt my cold, cold heart?
If I were a rose with thorns all around and you were a gentle hand
Would you pick me anyway?
If I were a star and you were a child
Would you make your first wish on me?
If I were the rain and you were the sun
Would you make us a rainbow?
If I were thunder and you were lightning
Would you light up the sky with me?
If I were the paper and you were the pen
Would you write us a love song?
If I were a woman lost and alone and you were a man
Would you take my hand and lead me home?
If I were, would you?

Kelly Shuler
Federal Heights, CO

Abundance

Having a friend is so clear
If able, share a tear
Overcome obstacles if you can
Shake burdens off shoulders of every man

Good and bad times occur as they may
But friends together will have their say
Converse with each other about struggles that may be
Focus on the positive as you can see

Trust and beauty are good qualities to have
They can make each other laugh
For whatever it's worth, friendship is full of care
Underneath, each is full of layers

Friends of long duration can rely on each other
We all look up to our mothers
We do not know what destiny can bring
It makes our friendship a fling

Beverly Cottam
Attleboro, MA

Poetry Written

Poetry written is easy to write and about
that I have come to give some divine insight.
It is a gift on the inside of you
that must be nurtured and released, too.
It is words written
and for me that is easy from where I am sittin'
your thoughts on paper, page after page,
that gets someone to read it with interest and get engaged
with its meaning, words of wisdom to receive
while gleaning there are a lot of poets
but they just don't know it,
not yet and my desire is to finish this poem and go "set."
I have been writing things and words that rhyme
for a very, very long time
and I can write poetry at the drop of a dime.
Poetry is a mystery given to man kind down through history.
To be able to read and enjoy and see
heartfelt sometimes sets the soul and spirit free
and this poem has been written by nobody like me!
So as I enter this poetry contest
may the reader of this word be blessed.

Earline Hagwood
Columbus, OH

Just Live

Don't try to go back
and relive your past
because you know at last,
we can never go back.

For sure don't worry
about the future.
It only holds endeavors
we all have to endure.

Just live every day
like it's your last.
You'll know tomorrow;
it just became your past.

Diane D. Christensen
Sioux Falls, SD

Thoughts After Cremation

My dearest, where are you?
Are you in the sweet smell of the wild flowers?
Or in the warmth of the morning sun?
Could you be there in the fragrance of the newly mowed grass?
I have searched everywhere since we've been apart.
Oh silly me, here you are, where you have always been:
Right here in my heart.

Margaret M. Whitlow
Wilmington, DE

My mother and father had four children. My sister, Ann, was the oldest and I the youngest. We were born in Scotland. I emigrated to the US when I was almost twenty (in 1956). My sister had the gift of intuition and she and I remained very close. She would write my name on a piece of paper and place it in her pocket. I, not knowing this, would call her from the US and would be amazed at this. She passed away almost five years ago. She was cremated and I would often pick up the phone just to talk to her. It left a void in my heart until I wrote the poem, "She is Always in My Heart."

English?

Isn't English strange?
We can see a saw
And ride a see saw
And pause for a moment
To wipe the dog's paws!
We can rake up the leaves
Or leave them there.
Or their? Or they're?
Is it your turn or you're?
Which two, to or too?
And why is it a tutu and
Not twotwo
or tootoo?
We know it's not Toto
But shouldn't that be Toetoe?
I get so confused!
Isn't English strange?!

Dorene Meaders
Bloomsburg, PA

Present

Sitting here thinking about the past
Don't know why it went by so fast
Was married with four kids
Awoke one morning to find love had hid
Away with my heart, my brain had seized
Couldn't think or even breathe
Now the kids are grown and grandkids appeared
My love and heart was surely seared
Burned and scared to no end
No more dancing with my friends
Love has surely flown like a coup
Disappeared like dense fog into thick soup
Alone I lay without a thought
Too tired even to be distraught

Florence Riddick
Barker, NY

Just a Reflection

I see a reflection of me,
inside a mirror.
Don't like what I see, so
I try to disappear.
All my life,
I have stayed the same.
As I grew old,
my priorities changed.
I wasted precious time
being a troubled, hard-headed girl,
missed out on a family, a good friendship
and love that will never have the chance to grow.
Feeling so ashamed
that my family is emotionally drained.
Makes me feel dead
because they feel pain
by the way I have behaved.

But before I let this reflection get the best of me,
I am going to get up
and put all dead ends to the ground
because this isn't me,
it's just a reflection that tries to use me!

Sarah Jones
Converse, TX

I'm Home Now

Can it really be? I've made it, happy day!
  I'm sorry my loved ones, but I had to go away.

Don't mourn my home-going and the life I led,
  Yet relish and celebrate it instead.

I pray we will see you again, Bryant and I,
  Only this time make our home on high.

How precious it is, the presence and peace I feel.
  It's here, it's there, close your eyes, reach out and feel!

Relish the fact that I am no longer in pain
  But I can shout, leap, and dance before the Lord again.

I know you all loved me and you know I loved you,
  So make plans to see me again and Bryant, too!

Chancy Reeves
Montgomery, LA

Seniors Sigh

"Just be nice, they are old,"
When we were young
We often were told.

So we pitied the Old Ones
And gave it no thought
That time on earth can never be bought.

And all too soon
We were the Aged—
Now we wanted to be noticed and praised.

We know it all better
Because we are wise
In fact—we want respect!
Our memories fail to include
How often, when young,
We were quite rude.

Alexandra H. Rodrigues
Massapequa, NY

*My childhood and youth were spent in turmoil during World War II. My
father was forced to flee from Berlin to Paris to avoid Nazi camps. For me,
it meant private tutoring and white lies. I worked as a sales clerk, typist,
secretary, and apprentice journalist. I spent two years in Sweden, a short
romance. In 1958, I was hired by Pan Am as a stewardess and set precedence
several times: in 1960, I initiated husband and wife cabin teams in flight. In
1965, I was among the first women to keep flight status after age thirty-two,
and in 1972, I was the first stewardess to return to flight after childbirth. I've
made thousands of notes and fantasized about being a writer. I have arrived!*

Missing Time

Time as we know it passes
on by, here today and gone before
you can blink an eye.
  So when something shocking
happens and changes your mind
you forget all about it in due
time.
  The missing time you thought
you had disappears out of sight.
  When can time bring it back
so you can see the light?
  There is no clue to think
about, your mind doesn't give it
a thought
  until one day in your plight
the missing time sorts it out.
  Now you found the missing
time, the answers are for you to
know.
  The past comes back to give
it up with a no-show.
  The answers are always
hidden out there, look and seek
and you will find the missing time.
  To be continued.

Mary S. Osborne
Jamestown, NY

The Day I Cry

Can I be me today
Not tomorrow but today
Can you see my soul
My life
My dreams
My hope
My world
My love
  You

Wesley D. Anderson
Port O'Connor, TX

Beneath the Shadowy Leaves

When I was a child, I played for hours beneath a big oak tree.
I'd spread an army blanket and serve my dollies tea.
And sometimes I would lay beneath the shadowy leaves,
partnered with the sun dancing on the breeze.
And oh, that soft summer wind, how gently it did blow
rising up my collar and flipping up my bow.
Then in a great big sigh, did draw them from my face,
tickling my nose like the very softest lace.
But now I am a grown girl with many matters to mind.
I fear not death, for in His love the peace of a child I'll find.

Sylvia LaBree
Roscoe, IL

How the Path Was Laid

Black smoke flirts with my eyelashes.
Ash kisses my forehead.
A warm halo falls to my ground.
Graceful flames entice my strength.
I have ignited my affliction.
My mind will not be riddled with fever again.
I had to set fire to my spirit, right before me.
The pain smoldering,
I hear the blaze eating the screams alive.
Now there is nothing left, not one breath.
I silence my inhalations and intently close my eyes,
Mindfully saluting my memories, finalizing the escape.
Suddenly, water rushes into every fiber,
Beginning at the crown of my head ending under the soles of my feet.
Cold whispers encompassing my energy.
Waves chase my scars away.
The flood seizes, I separate my bound, damp eyelids.
Lying before me, the ash united with water paving the earth.
Gracious is nature.
My intention is to utilize this union of charred and damp ground.
My journey begins
Upon the traces of fire and water.

Samantha O'Brien
Franklin, TN

Nature

Nature is one of the most beautiful things in the world
Nature is animals living peacefully in their warm, comfortable homes
Baby animals snuggling with their mothers and sleeping
Waterfalls falling into pools of crystal clear water
Butterflies flying to and fro everywhere
Nature is so beautiful, rain or shine
I even love the snow falling on the ground in the winter
The snow everywhere is perfect for building a snowman
My favorite part of nature is definitely the ocean with its sparkling waters
I love it when the sun shines down on the ocean to make it look so sparkly
I love it when the trees bear their juicy, delicious fruit
I love it when the leaves fall on the ground in the fall
It's so beautiful when the leaves change color
Spring is so beautiful with its flowers blooming everywhere
Nature is truly beautiful with its flowers, plants, oceans everywhere

Carolina Leon
Hollywood, FL

To Be Young

In your youth you don't very often feel the cold
and more often than not you wish to be old.
To be young is to be almost all worry-free—
not a care or concern just happy to be.

Toys are still a ton of good, clean fun
and your body feels great when you take off and run.
No debt, aches, or deadlines that cause you concern—
a video game victory is all you need discern.

At a young age you love your parents a bunch
but older and older toward a life of your own you feel the crunch.
Everything is cheery and happy and bright,
weights on your shoulders are airy and light.

Have fun and enjoy, run, play, have a blast—
your time as a child just goes by way too fast.
Don't waste even a moment from sunset til dawn
for in the blink of an eye your youth will be gone.

Skinned knees heal quickly and bruises they fade—
when the sun gets too hot you can play in the shade.
Slide, swing, climb monkey bars slow, rung by rung—
enjoy each and every moment of time while you're young.

Angela Sciriha
St Clair Shores, MI

The Summoning

The tears of the forgotten
Line the waters that run through
The folds of the glen
The greens veiled in dew

Summoned from the voids
Strangers that we are
Pilgrims chosen
To fight the good war

Gallant are we
Who raise the battle cries
The fight of the righteous
The wrath of sinful eyes

With the setting of the sun
In this sky of wintry white
Entombed in our minds:
"This will lead to paradise"

Karen T. Harter
Manhasset, NY

The Smile Through It All

You say to me. . ."You've changed"
You're not the same. . .
Right that you are. . .
I've been through it all. . .
life's ups and downs.
I am the same. . but,
I have changed.
I've grown stronger in this
Story of my life.
My loves have come and gone
Like the buds of a flower. . .
Blooming and falling from the
Stem when there is no more
Life to live. . but,
There are always more buds
For this flower in life. . .
Stronger, healthier, and
More wonderful than before.
With time, I will grow to love life
As it is. . I.have changed. . .
I'm not the same. . but,
I am still me. . .
The soul that you see. . .
The smile through it all.

Sheryn Scarborough
Seal Beach, CA

Tragic Death

Stop what you are doing, put down the phone, and stop mowing
The lawn, and be silent for five minutes—not one peep or whisper
Not one sound do I want to hear, keep the grass from growing,
All I ask is peace and quiet so I may say a few words on the
Tragic death of my wife:

My wife was the most beautiful person on earth
She was the wind that blew through my hair
Her skin was so soft and smooth and you could tell from just one glare.
She gave me meaning and purpose. There is no reason to surf
On a wave at the beach if she is not there.

There was no point in playing football if she was not
There to cheer me on. There was no point in doing
The cooking, cleaning, and washing the dishes and pots
If she was not there to help me do all of that.

I loved her; I cared about her, everything I did
Was for her. It was like I was a jar and she was the lid
And when you unscrew the lid and don't put it back on,
You lose it. I thank you for your peace and silence. Please
Go back to what you were doing and please pray that the tragic
Death of my wife was not in vain but that now she can rest in peace.

Danny Rigolini
Mocksville, NC

The Old Red Barn

In childhood memories, my mind can see
That the old red barn is a part of me.
With the youthful days of mud pies and baseballs
Comes the view of those four big, red walls.
Lifelong lessons we learned in the agricultural place
Like calves and puppies being born in this treasured space.
Our father would open the barn doors so we could walk through
Taking "giant" steps to keep up with him and holding hands, too.
Dad found a way to turn farm work into spontaneous fun. . .
He milked cows by hand and squirted cats one-by-one.
You could never forget the barnyard's strong rustic smell. . .
A part of our pleasant upbringing we all knew so well.
We climbed up crooked stairs to the haymow high,
And found simple joy watching pigeons fly by.
Jobs from sorting cows to throwing bales were hard work,
But happy times like ice skating in our own rink were a country "perk."
When we rode horseback all through the yard,
"Shut the barn doors!" warned Grandpa, our guard.
Right next to the barn where the chicken coop stood,
Mom taught us to gather eggs and to help when we could.
The strong structure survived all types of weather,
And influenced the lives of five siblings who grew up there together.
The old red barn. . a peaceful farm building with old-fashioned charm
Warms my heart with fond memories of the family farm.

Kim Pharis Weber
Groton, SD

*Growing up on the farm brought simple pleasures to our lives. We gained
so many valuable lifelong learning experiences through the years. This poem
was written by me for my parents. My siblings and I printed it on a picture of
us that was taken in front of the "old red barn," which is still standing today.
I wanted to include some of my memories from childhood for my parents to
thank them for helping me become the person I am today.*

The Bane of My Existence

1. Believing in a code of ethics
2. Believing that life is fair
3. Believing that people are honest
4. Believing in the Golden Rule
5. Believing that you are here for a reason
6. Believing that I am a good person
7. Believing in humanity
8. Believing that I am not alone in this world
9. Believing that I matter

If only I didn't believe in *the bane of my existence*

Jennifer Rice
Lacey, WA

My husband was the poet. He wrote me many love poems and he also wrote other poems. He would have entered this contest but he died. I am trying my hand at it now. This poem is the second poem I have written. The first one was a love poem to my husband that he asked me to write. He said, "You need to tell me why you love me and put it in a poem," so I did. That got me thinking, maybe I can write more poems. I have a few more in the works for fun.

My Collection

I have a collection of stars. I keep it in the sky.
I count them almost every night. They seem to multiply.

I collect the brilliant colors painted on the autumn leaves.
Perhaps you've seen this collection. I keep it in the trees.

I have many lovely seashells. I keep some along the shore.
The rest I keep in hiding along the ocean floor.

I sometimes collect snowflakes as they come floating down.
I watch them blend together like frosting on the ground.

I collect beautiful music, like the rhythm of the rain
As it does a little tap dance on my windowpane.

You ask how I keep such a collection, "Is it not a heavy toll?"
I answer, "No. It's easy. I keep it in my soul."

Marion Wrightington
Colchester, VT

Broken Kites

Broken kites don't fly in the sky,
Their tattered remains upon the ground lie.
Once they sailed high upon the dreams of a boy,
But of kites and dreams, both are destroyed.
Broken dolls won't open their eyes;
Through battered lips come their silent cries.
Once dressed in finery, it was a girl's best friend,
But baby dolls and friends have both met their end.
And what of the little girl and boy?
Where have they gone without their toys?
Never a chance was given to them,
The light in their eyes has grown very dim.
Now the sounds of war fall upon their ears.
Their life drains quietly through their tears.
Slowly their child-hopes will fade
As does all that man has made.

Pamela Hopkins
Conneaut, OH

I Am

I am responsible and interesting.
I wonder what Heaven looks like?
I hear the sound of the waves hitting the beach.
I see my aunt watching over me.
I want to be a game warden.

I am responsible and interesting.
I pretend that everybody chooses good over bad.
I feel people need to be fair.
I touch my family's heart.
I worry everybody will forget about the outdoors.
I cry when I think of my family members
who are no longer with me.

I am responsible and interesting.
I understand nobody lives forever.
I say that I'll choose good over bad.
I dream I have a good future.
I try to please everybody.
I hope to get a job.

I am responsible and interesting.

Maddy Hamman
Biggs, CA

The Day Passes

Her companion, the human one, wakes
Then shuffles down the dim hallway
Passing an upturned soft shoe
And a comb on the sink that failed
To tame her thin hair frazzled by the illness

Her cat, the Feline One, makes
Purring circles around legs of another
Whoring for food, he will give it anyway
Smelling coffee and browning bread
That no one will eat right now
As the day passes

Outside, the children focus on sidewalk
It leads them to the school yard
Under bare-branched maples on hard green ground
With no give or take
But he thinks, her roses will bloom anyway, soon
As the day passes

His hand is taken, held, squeezed, patted
He tells each one as they pass her
She will be missed and yes
Life will go on
Food will have taste
Music sound sweet
And laughter not choke him
As the day passes

Judy Laurinatis
Vandergirft, PA

When You Are Ninety

Now I am not a young chick,
I've had birthdays by the score.
My eyes are weak,
My knees creak,
My teeth come from the store.

But my, oh me,
You will see
If you'll give me a chance
You'll see what I can do—
I'll teach you how to dance.

One, two, three, four
One, two, three, four
Slide to the right and
Stomp the floor!

One, two, three four
One, two, three four
Clap your hands and
Out the door!

Gladys Y. Smith
Billings, MT

I am a retired RN. My inspiration occurs when randomly playing piano or riding horseback in the mountains of Colorado at Deer Valley Ranch.

A Change in the Night

alone at night
in your bed
you pull the covers
to hide your head
you burrow in your blankets deep inside
knowing that you can never truly hide
the boogeyman, the dream thief
he's come again
in your heart you feel he's here
to replace your dreams with your greatest fear
you feel his dark fingers reach
just about to grab your dreams
but tonight
is different it seems
you pull off the covers
reveal your face
he steps back truly amazed
yet you steel your eyes to meet his gaze
and here comes the moment he truly grieves
when you say those four little words:
"You don't scare me"
his eyes widen
he disappears like that
all that is left is a pile of ash
and now that you can finally be at peace
you lay down your head, close your eyes, and fall asleep. . .

Isabel Figueroa
Gainesville, VA

I'm a Fixer-Upper

I'm a fixer-upper
In need of much repair
Layer by layer stripped away
Til pride's no longer there

Room by room, restoration's on its way
To cleanse and renew
Til it's all shiny brand new

A place of beauty
A work of art
Waiting and praying
With all my heart

Shaped and molded
By the potter's hand
All according to His purpose and plan

I'm a fixer-upper
Needed much repair
No longer plain or ugly or bare

A sight to behold
Restoration complete
Each room a testament
To the carpenter extraordinaire!

The master's touch
Each piece in place
The journey over
Come now, enter His gates!

Connie Quintana
Canon City, CO

We live in a house built in the early 1900s. One day while remodeling the kitchen, I remember thinking that we are like these homes: different owners come and go, put their marks on a house to make it their own, and then new owners come in and rip things up, take things down, paint and repaint, etc., yet the house still stands. It parallels our lives. Through all the transitions we experience in life—birth, death, ups and downs of all kinds—we still stand. "Having done all, to stand." -Ephesians 6:13

Summertime

Summer has at last arrived
Makes us all feel alive

In the day the sun shines bright
And the stars sparkle in the sky at night

So much to do, time to get going
Hardly knowing what we're doing

Birds are singing and making nests
Bugs are coming around being pests

Green grass is growing
And will soon need mowing

Farmers are busy in the fields
Hoping for good yields

Be sure to make your time pay
And enjoy each and every day

Eileen Powers
Findlay, IL

Waiting

I am waiting for the green mornings,
the green fields of the young times.
I am waiting for the forest and the animals
to reclaim the earth
and the blessed meek to inherit it.

I am waiting for a refurbished Mayflower
to reach America
with a fresh scenario and TV rights.
I am waiting for a rebirth of wonder.

I am passionately waiting
to see God on television
not ostracized from it.
I am waiting for the right channel to tune in.

I especially await the secret of eternal youth
divulged by an obscure general practitioner.
I am waiting to write the indelible poem.
I am waiting for someone to really discover America.
I am waiting. . .
waiting for a rebirth of wonder.

Diana Gundrum
Nekoosa, WI

The Contest

I must write a poem
Just twenty-six lines long.
It's difficult since my thoughts
Speed ahead in rhythmic song.

There's so much to say,
How can I use so few words?
Only twenty-six little lines,
Well—it's simply absurd.

By the time I lay a plot
For what I wish to say,
My allotted lines have
All but passed away.

So I work and trim
Trying to keep the rhyme,
All the while thinking
My poor brain is working overtime.

At last looking it over
I've finally trimmed enough.
Believe it or not, what's left
Is just the right stuff.

Cherri Gallant
Columbia, CA

I'm turning the corner to my eightieth birthday. My husband and I had no children, but I have two awesome kids (entering their early senior years). I've been writing poetry for about thirty years (on and off, that is). I like writing about old people, kids, and my favorite: animals (especially my five awesome cats). I attribute my gift of writing poetry to Almighty God, and I include Him in most of my poems. I hope someday to have my poetry published.

Recycling Day

Everything unpacks
easily
from my green canvas tote.
Regrets here, aspirations
there and
promise just beyond
the corrugated.
Perhaps
I'll pick something up
while I'm here.
Amazing
what people throw away.

David Dillion
West Glover, VT

Mr. Dillon lives and writes in the Northeast Kingdom, Vermont town of East Albany.

My Brother. . .My Friend

Ever so many years ago, our dad always had a large garden spot;
He toiled, planted, then harvested in weather that was extremely hot.

In this garden, there were chosen the very best plots
Set aside for our famous family strawberry crops.

These tender plants needed very special care,
Whether the weather was stormy or beautifully fair.

Of these special-care duties, watering was what my brother and I got.
Too little water, the plants would die, and too much, they would rot.

To accomplish this daily watering task, a well was found
Away. . across a field of good pasture ground.

In due time our old pump was installed,
Then gallons and gallons of water, my brother and I hauled.

Oh, when the strawberries ripened, they were ever so great
And enjoyed by family and friends and all of us ate and ate.

Now, after so long, this is truly why
The old pump has special meaning, as the years have gone by.

To think that my brother, on one of my birthdays, worked so very hard
To make sure the pump was moved and placed in my front yard.

For this very difficult task that you undertook, moving each part,
I want to say, "Thank You, my brother," from the bottom of my heart!

Darlene Vaughn
Rantoul, IL

*Over the course of my lifetime, I have written a great number of poems. The
inspiration for much of this poetry is from my brother, my only sibling. In our
growing up years he was instrumental in creating new and adventurous ways to
keep us busy. Later we both grew up and now have our own families, but we
have remained very good friends. It is a privilege to honor him with this poem.*

Man of the Sea

As Man of the Sea,
I know how long my ship must be
from aft to bow,
mast to hull.

Man of the Sea
sails the seven seas
in search of the key
to unlock the treasures, unfree.

As Man of the Sea, neither Viking nor king,
swarthy pirate nor thief,
vow to lead my crew against all evil things
and smoke my cigar in peace.

My ship treads the water ocean to ocean,
dolphins and whales behind,
following: life has an order
and life on the seas will not cease.

I can still see the day
when I rest in the sea,
when the tide shall bring me out;
Man of the Sea, let me be.

Avast, with the rest of life ahead,
I will sail the remainder of sea,
above and across the blue
Forever as Man of the Sea!

Luke Jenkins
Griffin, GA

Your Mother's Wish

Remember me
When you comfort each other
Honor me
When you help each other
Celebrate me
When you visit each other
Love me
Through these, when I am gone
And you will always have
Your mother

Frances Jean Ontiveros-Squier
Aberdeen, NC

*This was written for the celebration of my grandmother, Paulina Munoz's
100th birthday. It honors all loving mothers including my own, Pauline Cortinas,
my four sisters, Chavela, Marty, Ruth, and Gloria, and my own five daughters,
Suzanna and Elena, who are mothers, and Carolina, Lizzie and Hannah.*

Gizmo

The wag of your tail is gone,
your bark I'll never hear again.
The clicking of your nails
is a thing of the past.
Looking at me with such
loving and devoted eyes
I only see in my dreams.
But, the love I still have
for you will always be
in my heart.
It will always be with
me forever.
You will always be with me.
I will always be with you.

Tina Velazquez
Sevierville, TN

My Uncle Tom

Uncle Tom, I knew him only a short while,
But he brought to me such a big smile.
So loving and gentle, for an uncle who's better?
He welcomed me to the family,
You'd never know I'd been gone forever.
He told me some stories, even a secret or two.
Some about me, maybe one about you.
When life took a turn, he vowed to fight to the end,
Hoping against hope he would somehow mend.
He fought and he fought 'til he could fight no more.
He walks now with loved ones gone before.
Now quiet and peaceful, not a care to be had;
For him to be there I am truly glad.
As he leaves us now, I won't be the same.
Still, for having known him, I'm glad that I came.

Pam Lovato
Frankfort, IN

The Road We Take

Am in final stage from youth to age, striving and driving on this road of life
My Passengers all told, family, friends new and old, and my mate, my late wife
The journey, each mile a most worthwhile ride with my bride at my side
Cherished memories from the trip packed in my grip and abide deeply inside
Not all roads driven, with directions given were as portrayed and well-paved; life's ups and downs, smiles and frowns, laughter and tears for years I braved
Some tolls, detours, potholes, fender-benders and rear-enders along the way; loss and grief, ill health and seeking relief, I must say, caused some dismay
Age brings a crucial stage to our deliberation in reaching our final destination; avoid the route of despair and doubt, select the road to elation and revelation
The road to *doom and gloom* lacks a reward to lead us forward out of sorrow; favor and savor the *road of hope and joy* for you to cope now and tomorrow
When this great trip is done and gone, a new glorious one will have just begun; through faith and belief, with great relief no more aims and games left undone
Will not be mistaken by the road taken, one of meetings and greetings and more; a blissful choice for this stirring event to rejoice with those who went before
The word of my Lord I will celebrate as we all congregate at Heaven's gate; forever together with my beloved wife, the love of my life, my mate, my fate

William R. Williams
Perrysburg, OH

I am a neophyte poet wannabe, no ego trip for me. Advising others how to cope is my intention and hope. By helping others, you see, it is really helping me. Wisdom comes with age—time to turn the page. I'm not looking for recognition but striving to stimulate cognition. Live your life as you will— here's my two cents from old Bill. Bill who? Octogenarian, veteran, graduate MS, retired health care administrator, father, grandfather, and widower— joker, sometimes. I play the cards I am dealt. I deeply miss my dear wife, but am making the best of my life—letting the sun shine in.

A Spider and Me—and Us

Waiting for a bus one day
I saw a tiny black spider
smaller than the pimple on my nose
climbing up a slippery wall
pausing briefly then to see
who it was who stopped in wonder
just to watch if it should fall
of course, that one was me

As I wondered looking up so high
what goal this creature sought
when choosing this dubious path
this wall so tall and shear
would it decide to continue or stop
or was it merely testing me
to see if I might come
and follow its lead to the very top?

The tiny spider would not let go
even though the bus was moving now
and thinking back as there I sat
I thought not quite out loud
As far as I could see
we are all that tiny black spider
and in the very same way
that tiny black spider was me

Arnold Marks
Philadelphia, PA

As I Look Out the Round Porthole

I see mountains of snow
Lakes of blue filled with ice
I feel close to You, dear Lord
I feel I'm in Your close presence
As we fly, the clouds start to open
Patches of greens, browns, roads, houses
Nuclear plant generating electricity
They seem so small, but to You, dear Lord,
Every living being has reverence
I feel I'm in Your close presence

I know the grief, the hunger, the loneliness
That is down there, I wish I could do
Something to eliminate the pain
Perhaps it is up to each individual to help themselves
Perhaps it is the test of the Ten Commandments
If we live by and obey them, I know we will
Always be in Your close presence

Betty Shlepr
Melbourne, FL

Light a Candle in the Window

Light a candle in the window for all the world to see.
Light a candle in the window, a sign of hope for you and me.

Light a candle in the window, the light will brightly shine.
Light a candle in the window to reassure us all will be fine.

Light a candle in the window, a symbol of the lives that we've lost.
Light a candle in the window and fight against the darkness at any cost.

Light a candle in the window, have your neighbor light one, too.
Light a candle in the window, with prayer and faith we will pull
through.

Barbara E. Smith
St. Clairsville, OH

What Would Jesus Do?

What would Jesus do if a man stood in the cold?
Would He turn His back and walk away
Or welcome him into the fold?

What would Jesus do if addictions upon a man came?
Would He show disgust and judge him harsh
Or console him through his weakness and shame?

What would Jesus do if a man dressed tattered and torn?
Would He find him worthless and cover him not
Or recall the rags He, too, had worn?

What would Jesus do if a man hungered in his strife?
Would He hoard His pantry and let him starve
Or would He feed him the bread of life?

What would Jesus do if a man lived in distrust and fear?
Would He dwell in His comfort and not ask why
Or share His Bible which shows God is near?

So what would Jesus think if His word we did not heed?
Would He question our faith and what's in our hearts
If we feel we are not loving the man in his need?

Elaine C. Savoy
Plainview, NY

My Dreams

Fell into sleep one rainy night
When mixing thoughts took wings of flight
By streets and hallways little light
Into a past of black and white

Old movies playing my dreams did spin
In fervent battle but not to win
One vivid scene to another begin
While traveling further then back again

As visions shifted through the trees
And tangled branches of memories
Or tossed on waves of turbulent seas
Erased by the wind of an ocean breeze

Still stirred I did between the lines
Of abstract thoughts of my design
Pictures painted time after time
The flashbacks recalled in my mind

Then I sank deeper into the night
To chase my thoughts on wings of flight
When came upon a fearful sight
Til up I woke at day's new light

Michael G. Schwartz
Bloomington, IL

Soon, Very Soon

Soon, very soon. . .
Our brother bear will vanish for the winter
And the cold rivers will flow on without him.
The spirit of quietness will walk the earth,
Leaving its trail in the air
With a cold, crisp and chilly feeling.
In a haunted sort of way,
While naked trees standing strong, their shadows
Are eerie, tall and wiry, moving strangely
On the ground to the whistling wind's strength
And force passing by.
Sunrise is more like sunset.
All across the sky and in through the clouds,
Shades of many colors change places,
Moving swiftly with the clouds.
Frost lies everywhere,
Sparkling like diamonds laid out
And scattered like valuable stones everywhere.
Crunching footsteps echoing with howling wolf clans
Searching hungrily for somebody to eat.
The days become darker sooner
As the mornings become darker longer.
Soon, very soon—
Winter will begin its story.

M. Margaret Hofseth
Marysville, WA

The Garden of Eden

It all began
Those many years ago
A perfect place
Two perfect souls

A man named Adam
A woman named Eve
A flawless land
Called the Garden of Eden

Beautiful flowers
Flowing streams
Birds singing
They had everything

Until that day
Clouds filled the sky
They didn't believe
The serpent had lied

It was just one fruit
An apple they say
To disobey God
And pay to this day

The tree of knowledge
The choice between good and evil
To know right from wrong
Is how you should have lived
All along!

Tony Ford
Edgewood, NM

I am a senior at Moriarty High School in Moriarty, NM. I wrote this poem my junior year in AP English when we were reading "East of Eden" and discussing good versus evil. I thought about where it all began and remembered how my dad always taught me how important it is to make the right choices in life. My parents and grandparents have always been there for me, and I know I am walking the right path in life.

The Marker

My love, come to me.
My grave is cold and unknown.
I lay here waiting, your Geri,
For you to put a marker where
There is none.

Unless friends are shown,
They do not know.
Soon they are gone.

The spirit of my soul cannot be free
Until you place a marker above me.

I cannot hurt you anymore.
My love, come to me, I implore
So my spirit can rest forever more.

Mary Mitckess
Kissimmee, FL

The poem is about my sister-in-law who loved poetry. As usual, every Wednesday a group of us would go to a lounge. But this one Wednesday, Geri refused to go with me. I begged her not to go with a friend of her's to Indiana. I had a very bad feeling that something bad would happen—and it did. Geri was killed in the car driven by her friend. Her husband refused to put a marker on her grave. Geri died on the eve of Thanksgiving in 1982.

My Family and Me

I had a talk with God today.
I asked him to help me along my way.
The sun is shining and it is cold,
I would like to take a walk if I wasn't so old.

God blessed me with a big family:
three boys, three girls, my husband and me.
Children grow up and they leave home,
they get married and have a family of their own.

I miss my children since they are gone,
and left me here all alone.
God gave me grandchildren to brighten my day,
they drop by to see me on their merry way.
They are always looking for something to eat,
'cause Grandma's cooking is hard to beat.

It's hard to imagine how life would be
Without my big family.

Frances C. Wagner
Kannapolis, NC

It Is Enough to Know

It is enough to know that if the hedge
Between us now were rent and torn apart,
You'd flee to me, as moth to flame, and pledge
Your liege on pain of death to win my heart.
Though we may never speak again or touch
Or know each other's souls and be consigned
Alone to dreams of life of being one—
Such would suffice, if fate be so unkind.

When life was spring, I craved it all and more,
But then my summer-sated heart grew wise—
When autumn came I took part fruit it bore
And did not mind at all the compromise.
Now winter's here with northwest wind and snow—
I do not feel the cold, it is enough to know.

Nina L. Ramsing
Beloit, WI

Still Me

Reflecting on my life, a bitter divorce
knocked me for a loop,
I survived.
A significant other becoming ill and dying—
I survived.
My ex-husband returning to help him
recover from an illness, I took care of him,
eventually he died. . .
I survived
Once more alone, I overcame hurdles to
see much joy, and now I play in a camp.
Like a child. . I.am free and wild,
Vibrant and strong. . still loving and kind
but never forgetting what I left behind.
Those memories will never fade, you see,
they are what they are and I am still me.

Judith Zuckerman
Boynton Beach, FL

Suddenly being alone and reflecting on my life, I now realize that the hardships and sorrows I had to endure helped to make me a stronger, better person. I had to share my story so others will know that with faith in themselves there is a brighter tomorrow.

How Like Love You Are

I had almost forgotten about you,
  But one spring morning you burst forth
From your flower cocoon
  And made my morning beautiful.

I tried to capture your elusiveness
  By gathering you to me,
But you closed your petals and withdrew yourself
  Out of my grasp.

And just when I thought you were gone forever,
  You burst forth again at dawn
With fresh blossoms
  Breathtaking as ever,
And drawing me once again
  Under your spell.

A wild flower you are,
  Full of mystery,
Adding elegance to the simple
  As you stand proudly by the busy roadside
Reminding me that beauty and love
  Can be found and relished
In the simple things.

As in love, I try to hold you,
  But once again, I find that I must wait
Until you come again to me!

Rosemary Fox
Hermitage, TN

I live in the beautiful state of Tennessee where we experience the unique beauty of the four seasons. Nature has always spoken to me in periods of happiness or challenges, and only poetry seemed to express what my heart felt. This poem was inspired by an event in the life of a daughter of ours as she struggled to find the love of her life. I hoped that these words would reassure her that love would come in its own time!

Time Gone By

A tear came rolling
down my face
   Thinking of the
world around us.
   It used to be so
simplified and now
what can you call it?
   It used to be the
town crier that once gave
us our news.
   Now, it's world
communication that
keeps us all in tune.
   Times were not as
prosperous or as golden
as today.
   Time goes by
and things do change;
   life will never
be the same.

Donna O'Grady
Warren, OH

Why?

When we first met
we seemed the same—
in heart and mind and soul.

Each new day was a blessing
as our love began to unfold.
The times we shared were filled
with laughter and fond memories.
Never did we foresee the day
of sadness and misery.

Yet, here we stand this day,
our lives seemed destined to part.
God in Heaven is the only one
that knows the pain that's in my heart.

I see your inner battles and understand
the choice you feel you must make.
I only hope that all of you
will prosper in its wake.

Who knows if we are right or wrong—
only time will tell.
But I give you this with all my love,
and sincerely wish all of you well!

Benny L. Hobden
Deweyville, TX

Untitled

I saw a child in
pain yet he or she
has nothing to gain, with
a disease like cancer
eating away.
But cancer can't stop
the smile of the day.
My heart cries and
aches for the child, that
doesn't know what's wrong
or what is going on inside.
But God whispers in
their ears, "Do not worry
little ones, I have you
right here in my arms."
You will stay, I know
there will be another day.

Peggy Thomas
Cincinnati, OH

What inspired me to write this poem was children that have cancer, the children I see on television from the St. Jude commercial. The children hurt and ache. My heart cries for them because they don't know what's going on in their little bodies. They are frightened, the little ones don't know what's going to happen to them next. I always wanted to go and visit these children, that is my dream. I am a mother of four. I have just retired in June of this year. They are in my hearts, may God bless all children.

I Wonder

I wonder as I walk along the shore
If someone walked these sands before, wondering.

I wonder if it was ever so that hidden treasures lay below,
buried by the sand and time, leaving thoughts to wondering
minds like mine.

I wonder if the sad and lonely walked the shores like me,
crying out their hearts with tears to the rolling sea.

I wonder if those who walked before me cleansed their minds and
souls,
Giving them a new tomorrow to reach their dreamed-of goals.

I wonder as I leave the quiet and unending peace of mind,
Will I return to life fulfilled and reach that star of mine?

Margaret S. Pohjola
Wakefield, MI

My Dog

She isn't asking to take a walk
  Looking at me with big brown eyes
No matter what my soulful talk
  She always seems to sympathize

There's kindness in her knowing look
  That somehow brightens the day
Words can sometimes be mistook
  What does understanding say?

Caring for one another, dog to man
  Or man to his "best friend"
Although her "tag" is a toy-maker's brand,
  What a message those eyes send

That's *Bitsey*

Poet Stuart
Stow, OH

Old Boots

My boots are worn and battered
As they stand outside the door,
Caked with years of dirt and grime
They can't come in anymore.

We tramped the hills together
Those run-down boots and I,
We forded streams and muddy spots—
On them I could rely.

They protected me from things that cut
And from snakes that creep along;
Discolored with the leather cracked,
Their heels are scarred and worn.

A brand new pair of hand-sewn boots
Are in my closet now,
Clean and smooth and shiny bright,
They seem all wrong somehow.

The old boots are a part of me
They've been around so long,
And I will surely miss them
Someday when they are gone.

Norma Stephen
Weaverville, NC

One More Ride

Just *west* of the North Pole
Is a very large hole
Containing a huge bag
That would make your back sag

East of the hole stood four old deer
Knowing for sure the "big night" was near
They knew the big bag was loaded with toys
Dolls for the girls and bikes for the boys

But now they're retired and, man, are they glad
Because those sweet little tykes have all turned bad
The scars on their hides was plenty of proof
They would never set hoof on another roof

Now Santa was standing just *south* of all that
Dressed up in his red suit and new Santa hat
The sleigh was all polished and ready to go
The packages were wrapped and tied with a bow

His new herd of reindeer had all been trained
And was ready to be fed, harnessed and reined
When suddenly they got nervous and ran away
Leaving Santa with no deer to pull his big sleigh

Then all of a sudden he heard thundering hooves
Coming straight from the *north* jumping over the roofs
The old retired herd nuzzled up to his side
And said, "Come on Santa—let's take one more ride!"

Betty J. Staley
Sun City West, AZ

One by One

I sit alone in the field as the sun warms my face
The wind softly whistles through the tall stalks of grass and combs
through my long blonde hair
Each strand, one by one
A gray bird with a bright red head lands on the sun-warmed earth
And he chirps a cheerful melody
Each note, one by one
The clouds twist and contort their shape forming new things
Each minute, each hour, each day
I watch as they each roll by, one by one
Soon the white clouds start to turn a charcoal shade of gray
And raindrops start to fall
Each drop, one by one
Lightning rips across the sky
Soon followed by rumbling thunder
Each bolt, one by one
"Better get inside," I think as I get up from the grass that so warmly
welcomed me
And I start dancing towards the house
Each step, one by one

Jenny Thompson
Omaha, NE

Low Down Windshield Wiper Blues

Woke up this morning, start of a new day
Gotta get to work, so outta my way
Slid into the old Ford, cranked the engine over
and purr it did, just like the cat I named Clover
better get out of this joint,
'cause if I'm late, gonna get docked another point.
Too many points won't have a job at all,
that's another story so I'll save it for the fall
Oh, for goodness sake, can't believe it's raining
better turn the wipers on for my eyes are a-straining
What, this can't be real.
Wipers aren't working, this is a big deal.
Man, now I'm starting to feel those low down windshield wiper blues.
Pulled over to the side of the road, come on wipers, prove to be true
'cause now time is really overdue.
Yes! I hear a connection,
oh, do hurry, set me in the right direction.
Thank you, thank you, keep on wiping,
gotta get to work so I can start typing.
Look! Up ahead there's the roadwork crew,
at least there's no more windshield wiper blues.
That was a close call and it really sucked
just goes to show, what rotten luck.
Can't feel too sorry though.
The work crew guys working in the rain,
I now believe that's the biggest pain. . .

Renea M. Rehbein
Circle Pines, MN

Mom

Oh Mom, I love you
Why couldn't you stay—even just for a few more days?
There was so much more I wanted to say
Although I'm glad you're no longer suffering—you're in God's care,
It's just not fair
Your life was hard—
So many obstacles to overcome
So many things we were going to do—
But putting it off was all we would do
Although you passed away—you're alive in my everyday
My looks, my knowledge, the way you raised me
It will never fade away
I know when it's my time
You will be there to guide me with open arms
But til that day, I just want to say,
I love you, Mom

Janet LoRusso
Mount Vernon, NY

Beautiful New York City

New York, New York, what a lovely city
New York, New York, you're so dear to me
A city so full of fun
It's so nice to walk around
Beautiful things to see and do

What I'm saying is true
You could ride the subway all day
At night enjoy neon lights
Choose any game to watch
Wide variety of food to eat
Oh, what a treat

New York City is so nice
They had to name you twice
What a fun place to be

A trip to Broadway goes a long way
There's no place I'd rather be
New York, New York, you made my day
On my next visit I decided to stay

Theophilus Roome
Newark, NJ

The Sight of Memories

Her sight was gone now,
lost to a cruel disease.
But her memories were clear.
Projected for her alone to see—
scurrying clouds in azure skies;
waves that drained the ocean;
first buds of spring; fiery colors of fall;
filmy faces of lost loves.
Sometimes the images came with sounds
and sometimes with scents.
Those senses were sharper now.
Often, she would laugh to herself
causing concern to outsiders.
She was selfishly and curiously content
with the slide show in her mind.
She shared it with no-one.

Heather Russell
Florence, AL

*My recently acquired interest in writing poetry was inspired and encouraged
by Dr. Dorothy Hardy at her "Intergenerational Writing Class."*

Crystallized Memories

When one dark crystallized night,
    far into the future,
    you lie awake
    unable to sleep
    and memories slowly creep. . .
    into your consciousness,
Bittersweet memories,
    of a time shared by me and you,
    and against your will
    you shiver with remembered lust—
I trust
    that sadness will fill your unrested spirit
    and restlessness will recut throughout the night
    because still you're not satisfied with your life. . .
Look back—with regret—
    and see my face and mind
    for which you had no time
    and know you'll always wonder why

Charlene Nuti
Itasca, IL

The Destroyer

The devil is a liar—a truth he cannot tell
He once lived in Heaven but soon will live in hell
He whispers in your ear and tries to lead you astray
If you're a Christian—he will visit you every day
He's not good company so I won't let him stay
I open my door and I tell him—you won't get me down
So you take your lies and you get out of town
He must remember the promise I made to my Lord and Savior some ten
years ago,
So he works real hard and we go nose to nose
But he must remember that I pray to my Father and He keeps me on my
toes
He can't work hard enough to completely get me down
I'm going up—I refuse to go down
Because of my Father's Son going on the Cross
My soul will not be lost

Anna Richard
Taylor, MI

Gramma

Long hair braided
Color of the sun
Bare feet calloused and brown
    from years of hoeing and
    working the ground

Shorts and tee, her
    usual dress

Head to the garden
    to fix the mess

Pull the weeds, cuss at
    the grass that won't
    give up growing in
    the berry patch

Head to the house
    old man will be here soon
    looking for his meal at noon

Need a day off

Days done, bed feels good
    she sleeps sound
    waits for another day
    to come around

Such is her life, been
    so for years,
No change, just days

She wouldn't have it
    any other way

Jackie Geldersma
Sidney, MI

Reality from a Dream Is Born

How great to know a boy of four
Who opens up forgotten doors
Through whose eyes a grown-up sees
The forgotten world of make-believe
Leaves for a while this world of care
For fairy castles in the air
Takes us on a magic carpet of dreams
Where we can see all sorts of things
No place is too near or far
Stand on our toes and touch a star
But—don't we grown-ups possess such vision
Coupled with foresight and matured with wisdom
We send men out to touch far planets unseen
And keep in our hearts the childhood dream

Elizabeth Thompson
Blandburg, PA

Country Concerto

The hushed arpeggio of the leaves
Waked me from an early dream
The wind swept a rushing stream
Soft music in the early morn
No other sounds broke this score
But the birds whose morning wing
Brought staccato notes needed in this theme

I have not heard another round
That means more to me than this sound
It's nature's way in breaking day
Symphonic themes to start this way
Forming a concerto already in play

Natalia Tanner-Cain
Southfield, MI

I am a semi-retired pediatrician with a subspecialty in adolescent medicine. I have enjoyed a long and distinguished career. I have been a writer since early childhood inspired by nature, music, art, and my family. In high school I was elected to the International Society for High School Journalists "Quid Nunc." I have published scientific data, but I have not submitted other writings for publication. At present, I am writing my memoirs, "The Black Side of the White Coat," which will be submitted for publication in 2014. I enjoyed a long-term, happy marriage of sixty-four years to a prominent surgeon. Our marriage produced two daughters, one a lawyer and one a physician.

Peace

I want to go far, far, far
away,
where no one knows
who I am or
who I might have been.

Where is peace
and where do you find it?
Peace from birth-destroyed
and peace with death.

Peace with words
spoken from silence of the lips.

Does peace flow in and out
or does it come within
and find a resting place
that never lets go of your
mind, body, or soul?

Spirit of peace—*dove.*
Can we or should we
not forget
Jesus promises or promised us
perfect peace?

Vailoree C. Stevenson
New York, NY

For the Brother and Sisters

Wouldn't it be fun if we could
Turn back the clock today,
And see ourselves as children
When our hearts were young and gay?

We never had to worry, and
Our futures looked so bright.
We made a lot of choices,
Sometimes we chose just right.

Come along and look back in time
And for a moment, see
Us playing ball, or tag, or dolls.
We were happy as could be.

The time slipped by and
We rushed back to and fro,
And now we are the *elders*!
Where on earth did the time go?

Never mind yesterday, and
Forget about tomorrow.
Live just for today and keep in mind,
Time is something you can't borrow.

Make every moment count
As you travel on your way.
Trust God to bless you always
Through each night and through each day!

Olive King
Lawrenceville, GA

I have written over one hundred poems in the last few years, mostly to my family, friends, and acquaintances who need encouragement when life becomes full of sorrow and great pain. I remind them that no matter what circumstances come to us, our Lord has promised that He will always be with us and never forsake us. Faith in His word can pull us through absolutely anything when there is nowhere else to turn. It works for me and can work for anyone who can truly turn their heartaches over to Him and not take them back again.

Sisters

We started out as the girls of four
and now we are down to two:
just me and you.
We are getting old and worn out,
but we laugh at each other, that is what we are all about.
We have had our ups and downs as sisters do,
but our love for each other always comes through.
And now we find that you, my sister, is ill.
We are hoping that you can be healed with a certain pill.
The doctors say your age is against you and that is a scare.
To lose you now, I couldn't bear.
But your outlook is good and your humor we share.
You are going to beat this because we all care.
Each day we would sit on the porch and talk
about the problems of the world
And quietly just look across the way,
then someone would come by and say,
"What are you looking for today?"
We just laugh and say,"Just looking, haven't found it yet,"
but one day we will, you can bet.
Now she is gone, her body was tired and it gave way,
but now as I sit here alone, I hear her whisper and say,
"Sis, I finally found it today."

Milly J. Harper
Mauriceville, TX

A Wild Child

I saw a wild child
sitting by the road.
He would not look at me,
I could tell he had a heavy load.

His eyes were sad and gloomy,
he felt he had no worth.
His roots to life were stunted
by the rudeness of people
on this earth.

In some strange way, the
boy's plight touched a place in me
So deep—that I shed tears of
compassion on him while he lay
there asleep.

What joy for me to see him now
opening his blue eyes and nodding
with a knowing smile—each time
I pass him by—

Remember, the environment
Shapes the way people grow
and when they discover what
love means—when God's love
to them you show.

Tia Marie
Quinton, VA

Mother's Love

She walked in beauty. . .
Tall, stately, lovely. . .
Her hair—shining and black,
Her skin—pale and smooth,
Her eyes—rich, dark and brown.

She gentled all. . .
   Touching and loving were her virtues. . .

My mother, a listener. . .
   As I complained about the kid
   That poked me—and on and on. . .

Her wisdom soothed my heart
   And nurtured my soul.

Love was her mantra. . .
   The Lord—her lover and soul-mate.

Rest in peace, Mom.

Stephania Walczak
Rochester, NY

My poem, entitled "Mother's Love," was inspired by my dear mother who died in 1968. I have been writing verse since the 1970s, but only became serious about it as I reached my eighties. This year particularly, as I celebrate my 60th Jubilee Year as a religious sister of the School Sisters of Notre Dame of the Atlantic-Midwest province, my passion for expressing myself in verse has dominated my thoughts and spirit. I have been an English teacher at high school for the past forty-plus years (now semi-retired).

The Two Trumpets

As I stand at the window
of my second-story room,
I can almost feel the winds
tugging at the balloons of red and gold
fastened to the dark, black branches
of the trees.

On the other side of the park
I know there is freshly spaded earth,
shiny and black,
whose mouth has swallowed my love,
my light,
leaving stark, hollow emptiness within me.

I watch a leaf slowly swirl to the ground—
like me, detached from reality.
I hear again the last trumpet note.
Taps.

My mind reminds me
there will be another trumpet—
triumphantly shattering the mounds
of rampant, overgrown grasses.

But today
my heart hugs its hurt
and knows only sorrow—
and loneliness.

Sunny Powers
Ames, IA

*When my friend's daughter was ready to marry, her Marine boyfriend was
sent overseas and was killed by a sniper just eleven days later. When they
played taps at the funeral, it just broke my heart to see her grieve at such a
young age. We are Christians; we believe Jesus will come, as the Bible says,
with the trumpet of God and the dead believers will be raised from their
graves. That is a comfort to us, but I knew at that time, she just wanted to
hug herself and grieve her loss. This poem was for her.*

The Big 4-0

So you're celebrating your 40th
It's really not that bad
It's the ones that follow later
That make you feel so sad
You'll have to iron your face one day,
Instead of ironing clothes
You'll wear supports of every kind
And everybody knows
Your hair turns gray, your teeth fall out
Your boobs drag on the floor
And what you see in the mirror one day
Was not in there before
Your eyes can't see, your ears can't hear
Your knees won't work, and then. . .
You'll think about this birthday
And only to be forty again!

Trudy A. Young
Lancaster, OH

The Visitor

I saw him this morning, down by the lake,
Thought how handsome, though a bit overweight,
Then he strolled quite close to my patio door,
A stranger, I had never seen before.

Was he lost? Trespassing on our ground,
Seeming bewildered as he looked around
Then quickly looking from left to right,
He appeared to be in quite a fright.

But he hung around for quite a while,
And as I watched I had to smile,
So wanting to get a better look,
I opened the door, but off he took.

Back to the lake, he hurried that day,
And with one last look, *the duck* swam away.

Virginia Henry
Dunellen, NJ

I am now eighty-nine years old, but I remember clearly the first four lines I put together in rhyme in second grade. Through the years I have enjoyed jotting down my feelings, inspirations, and heartfelt experiences in simple verse. This poem was a true experience and also tells a little story.

Bitter Acts of War

A young warrior stands—care in his heart
A patriot to his core
He leads as he follows; cool—smart
A warrior on tour

His country he will protect as nothing else matters
Except the precious family he left behind
With hopes the memory of him will not shatter
But he knows they will wait for him aligned

Try as they might, the warriors know that hands are tied
From the fierce enemy that has guns, IEDs and knives
With hidden devices, these enemy soldiers that hide
But the warrior is there to protect, to teach, to stay alive

He's always known this was his to do
He knows in his heart he is destined
Which lights a fire and his faith anew
For this he has never questioned
There's something in the future that is his due

But his brothers killed in combat he will avenge
It all matters to this warrior: protecting his country
His family, his friends

His destiny is home in Oregon in the end
With the subtle breeze in his hair
Without the horrors of a people who do not bend
The aroma of the warm grass in his own lair
And the peace of this land to tend
Far from the *bitter acts of war*

Aloha Riley
Grants Pass, OR

The Legacy

As we walk here in the sun,
we wonder about our lives to come.
Knowing that one day we shall die,
will we leave mankind something to remember us by?
Is it important for a man to leave a legacy
of something grand?
Not of worldly treasures or sound advice,
but doing good deeds sounds so nice.
Deeds done in a manner good-hearted
can neither be bought, sold nor bartered.
Such help we can give one another,
no cost, no fee, just the love of a brother.
The good deeds one does for folks
are the memories one remembers the most.
A legacy like this which is left behind
is such that we will leave mankind.
Knowing this is now our thoughts,
we'll do these deeds that can't be bought.
Our love for man shall now proceed—
not just thinking but doing these deeds!
Then upon dying and leaving this life,
we'll know that some have had less strife
by giving them something more precious than gold:
brotherly love which can't be bought or sold.

Helen P. Miller
Harrisonburg, VA

I am an eighty-five-year-old mother of five children and just celebrated my sixty-fifth wedding anniversary on July 18, 2013. I was raised by my grandmother who taught me to always be a caring person to everyone. Thus, all my life I've been a helper to people of all ages and all nationalities. Any deed, no matter how small, that helps another has always been my goal. Yes, brotherly love is not bought or sold; it comes from one's heart.

Don't Be a Nick

Hey there, sucker and lonesome loser
Girls won't pucker if you're a tobacco user
The ladies love tall men who smell fresh and clean
They don't want a small man like Nick O'Tine

As you can see, smoking has stunted Nick's growth
Filling his lungs with tar while choking his throat
His clothes all reek and his breath is stale
His body feels weak and his health is frail

But he thinks it's hot to light up a Kool
He does this a lot to get him through school
You won't find him dating any honies or having sex
'Cause he spends all his money buying cigarettes

When he was born he was cute, they all said
But now he's got horns growing out of his head
So take my advice and you won't end up like Nick
Don't think twice and put out that cancer stick

Carl A. Weaver
Glenview, IL

A Poem of Old Ends and New Beginnings

At last the clock strikes its last chime
And the flowers wither away to the earth
And the curtain closes on the final show
Yet for every sunset, there is a sunrise
And for every cold winter, a spring of life
And for every time of despair, a reason to hope

And for all the separations we face
The bonds we forge remain in our hearts
And we will carry them forever
All the love we share
All the good times we have had together
All those who have gone before, never forgotten

We have been one in our joy
One in our grief, our anger, our strife, and our pain
One in all we have done
And so, as we forge new bonds
And spark new fires
And let the sun rise on the dawn of new days
We shall hold fast in our memory
And hold onto them in our hearts
Til death do us part

John Rigolizzo
Berlin, NJ

In the Skies Above

Clear blue and yellow sunny skies
Captivate my wondering thoughts,
Holding me hostage peacefully
In the skies above.

White clouds pass over me,
Disguised as creatures in cotton imagery,
Dancing, prancing, moving silently
In the skies above.

Orange sunsets ablaze with wonder
As a fireball of mystery,
Illuminating the world before its *good-night*
In the skies above.

Gray, thunderous days speak,
Calling to us with flashes of lightning,
Demanding our full attention
In the skies above.

Joyce Glenn
Bronx, NY

Kim Louise Rebh

Kind and considerate, that's what you are
Independent and helpful makes you a star
Marvelous at everything you do

Loyalty and trust gives five stars to you
Optimistic, you take things in stride
Utilizes time, and has lots of pride
Is not a pessimist. . sees things as they are
Surely you have earned another star
Excellent you are, ask your best pal

Results add up to a very special gal
Excels in each and every endeavor
Beauty you have and are also quite clever
Humorous, that is your style
And
You know how to make everyone smile

Loretta F. Rebh
White Lake, MI

To a Son, from a Father

You'll become everything I never was
Down the line and into dust
Be all I am and all God does
One day, when our gold turns to rust
You will carry on, young one,
An image-bearing son of love
When all of us are dead and gone,
We grant you wings to fly above
This future is not about legacy,
But of love, fortune, and good will to all
Spread the word for all to see,
Watch your step because all must fall
Child, listen close to this proverb,
The world will try to cause you strife
Throw out the world to the curb,
Join God's fight for eternal life

William Hubbard
Beaverton, OR

Once We

Once we
spoke young.
Once we
ran innocent.
Once we
trusted. But
once we
broke vows.
Once we
fell fragile.
Once we
stared steady.
Once we
clung jealously.
Once we
tried. Just
once we
faltered. That
once we
died.
Once.

Jennah Sue Kelley
Bemidji, MN

Eternal

Wind strums the pages of my book. The beetle
coated with baked apples
struggles to hold on to the loops of the *os*,
the hooks of the *gs*.
Grabs at
nothing but the unforgiving
slip of a page. A dandelion
that stained page fifty-three for two and a half
decades drifts off the tumbling

pages. Cartwheels into the
faded green of grass. The front cover,
worn into ashes, threads over seams
sliced away. Knife into

butter. The book unravels like a bundle of
yarn. Pages torn, words fumbled, chapters dancing around
the film of dust that lacquers the corners
of the scraped wooden porch.

When I return from the
kitchen, jam tart crumbling in the sugared palm of my hand,
I walk to the book. No. To the pages. Not even. To the
three words that just stare back, that

happen to mean
everything:

". . I.love you."

Mihika Kapoor
Scarsdale, NY

These Green Eyes

These green eyes
Are turning red tonight.
Sober up
And cry on the shoulder of a stranger.
Have your eyes felt tears for me?
Is that possible, possibly?
Or am I just a forgotten memory?
Bring back the love tonight.
Find the joy in these hopeless eyes
And maybe I'll put on a disguise.
If your heart has no room for me,
Unlock the door and set me free
And I'll forever hold the key.
Maybe you loved me once.
Maybe you just had a crush,
But whatever it was,
It only lasted a couple months.
Hold on to these memories.
Hold on forever, please,
And I'll never forget you.
I guarantee.

Jade Spilka
Hendersonville, TN

Shaving

The clipper cannon's silent now,
The artillery has done its job well
The enemy lies in shreds, cut down without mercy. . .
But they are not dead yet

The grief comes to the ones that are clever
They bunker down in the cleft, in cupid's arch. . .
Our heavy firepower, our preliminary assaults,
They don't even touch the bastards; the ones that dig in deep,
They're the ones for the commandos, the specialists

Nothing for them but to send forces
Directly into those hellish nests and they're waiting for us
They're always waiting for us
Getting there's hard enough, but once we get in. . chaos
Tight space, no room to maneuver, nowhere to retreat
Tension, chaos, friendly fire, and blood
So unlike the clean precision of the earlier waves

Sometimes, I think they're laughing at us as they die
So many of us go into those hellish nooks
So few of us come out and the ones that do
Only have a short future to look forward to
Before the next war, the next time they are called in

We've seen so much blood, and it doesn't matter
How many times you staunch the flow with tissue paper
There will always be more—in a day, in a week. . .
In the end, it doesn't matter—our lot is never-ending war
Because the bastards always come back
They are not dead yet, they will never be dead

Nicholas Theodore Ogburn
St Johns, FL

This literally came to me after a long battle of shaving my face. I thought, "My, this is a real battle." The rest came naturally.

Once Upon a Time

I ask myself...
Who will come?
The past and the present answer:
    No one.
No one will ever come.
You must smile. Smile and look in good spirits...
This feeling is empty...
My happiness is jaded.
Laughing.
Smiling...
Not right.
Never think about it.
Once you think, it will stop. You will end.
    Alone. *Never again.*
So imagine "Once Upon a Time" until you break,
The pieces falling. Sounds Like a tree.
The one unheard.
I know. I will disappear.
I have always known.
Desperate to hold.
To push away.
That pretend to see me,
That pretend to care
And can watch me burn.
I pretend to be seen and not notice.
    Out.
No words describe nothing better.

Tamera L. Coffer
Fresno, CA

Killing My Willoughby

When I kill my Willoughby
I will sing a country dance,
sweetly stealing all his breath.
I will saunter up to him,
moving oh, so rhythmically,
two-stepping towards his grave.
Quick-quick, slow, slow, quick-quick.

When they bury Willoughby,
I will wear no widow's weeds.
Lacy black is for the wife.
I will hear the eulogy
without a single tear.
Stone-faced I will recollect
the dance that brought him here.

Quick-quick, slow, slow, quick-quick.

Spring Pearson
Asheville, NC

You Are The One

You are the one
Says my heart
You are as beautiful as the sun
When it sets. A true masterpiece of art
Your heavenly brown eyes
Comfort me
I feel like I can rise
To the stars, but you are the closest to heaven that I'll ever be

The sight of you makes my day, even on days that are grey
You are the nicest and sweetest person that I have ever seen
I think what we could have been
You have been in relationships with guys that are mean
To you and make you cry, I believe that is a sin

Brandon Micheal Roulette
Independence, MO

Crystal Meth, the Monster Drug Will Eat Your Soul!

My heart is breaking
I can't remember when it hurt so much
A monster has taken my daughter from me
It's a big monster, bigger than anything I could ever imagine
This monster is squeezing the life out of my beautiful daughter
I can't help her, she won't let me
She only has eyes for the monster
I can't get her to see me, how much I love her,
How much I want her back the way she used to be

Judith M. Yates
East Wenatchee, WA

Again!

Where have you gone, where have you been?
I've been waiting all my life to see you again.
You've let me down, baby, once or twice.
Now I have lost count and I want to say goodbye!
You've got me now under a spell.
Just leave me alone, baby, I'm not well.
I don't want to talk, I don't want to offend anyone.
To see you again my heart will never mend.
I will, never again, love you again.
To see you again!

Tayler Nelson
Westby, WI

Life

Life is an everlasting fire
just swaying to and fro,

it has no place to travel, nor no place to go.

Death is a burned-out candle,
it has had its time,

and its burning light of life will no longer shine.

Love is light rain,

it sprinkles pain here and there,

but around it a rainbow shines that will leave you no despair.

Megan Lowry-Smith
Bobcaygeon, ON

Injustice

February, 2012: Trayvon Martin was killed,
Reminds me of back in '55, what happened to Emmett Till.
Killer fighting for justice knowing he's the reason Trayvon's dead,
Milam didn't care when he shot Emmett in the head.
Trayvon had Skittles and Arizona,
Emmett had his father's ring.
The suspects claim self-defense
When no harm can be committed by these things.
Milam and Bryant took Emmett from where he stayed,
At the bottom of the Tallahassee River was where his body laid.
Can't forget Raynard Johnson who was hung from a tree;
People are getting killed just for liking what they see.
Trayvon Martin on the ground,
Pronounced dead at the scene, with no pulse and no sound.
We're supposed to be united, we're supposed to be a team.
We're supposed to live the life Dr. Martin saw in his dream.

Kambria Michelle Jolly-Harris
Wilson, NC

All My Powers

I feel happiness
I wish to sing along
Happy with power
I feel strength in me
Mentally and physically
Nothing can stop me

I feel the wisdom
Just my immature wisdom
But I live by it

Ava Sophia Fan
Fort Assiniboine, AB

Central America

The countries of Central America constitute the physique of a beautiful
woman.
Costa Rica and Panama are her inferior extremities.
Nicaragua and Honduras form the waist of this divine woman.
Buried in El Salvador is the heart, and by Jiquilico Bay her breast.
Her hair forms Guatemala which falls over Nicaragua. Her face so
pretty with
Birthmarks beneath her mouth. It is the figure of an angel from Central
America I always fall in love with.

Julian Hernandez
Union City, NJ

Shame

A devastating, white-hot heat
Radiating from my pores,
Darkness, my stomach and mouth
Filled with mold and moss,
Pupils swelling to the size of sockets
Murky as big, black thunder clouds
From such a great distance
With sticky, moist breath on the nape of my neck,
Every fiber, hair, small—insignificant
Particle standing in a scared salute
Two hands emerge, one covers my mouth
My nose, slowly forcing stale,
Menacing air in and out of my
Lungs without reprieve,
The other searching my breath
For my weaknesses
The areas of my person that
Flee, freeze, or fly sparked by
The mere grace of a fingertip
Slow, steady, damp splotches:
Acid oozing from black holes,
Burning my cheeks,
I turn towards the fire
My eyes wide open,
A disturbing realization
One is certainly the hand of a stranger,
The other, sad cruel truth,
Is my own

Sarah Heath
Denver, CO

A Fallen Idol

Bane. . that is all that I have of a name
Bereft of meaning. . sodden in shame
For I have sinned sinners' sins
And can't recall where to begin
My saga. . my burden
I was born in a time of drought
A time of worry, a time of doubt
A child not sown from the seeds of passion
But from violence and guilt
It's from these I was fashioned
By the time I knew my right from wrong
I knew too well it was wrong that was strong
So I did unto others as was done unto me
All along
Whelped by fear, nursed by the dark
No idol to speak of, no light, no spark
I became the black in the black of the night
And I grew from frightened into fright
I am what sneaks up behind
I am that nagging thought
I am that fear that you fear
You thought you forgot
Or regretted
As I once too regretted even myself
Bane. . that is all that I have of a name
But I have you my lovely
In mind

Joel Clark Linderoth
San Francisco, CA

If you like "A Fallen Idol," please consider ordering my self-published collection of ten children's poems entitled Almost & Always. *The poems are parables containing moral lessons derived from characters' names. My hope is that the poems create a dialogue between parents and children, teachers and students, about the underlying message. The writing style pays homage to Shel Silverstein—one of the most gifted poets at bridging the gap between young and old. My poems are available at https://www.createspace.com/4175136.*

Me, Not a Show

It's a way to show
I'm just being me
I'm not putting on a show
I'm just being true to me
not being low
and not trying to be
anything that you need to know
I'm just being me
trying not to glow
if you don't like me
by all means, then, just blow
away from me
because I don't want to know
who you are
now you mean
nothing to me

Kayla Harvey
Livonia, NY

This poem was inspired by me not being able to stand up for myself in high school. It was hard, but once I did, I was a lot happier. I just want everyone to know that it's okay to be different. I am grateful for it though, because I wouldn't be the person I am today. My inspiration comes from my favorite artist, Eminem. He has inspired me so much to be myself. I would like to take this time out to thank my family. They mean the world to me, I love all of them so much.

Friend Zone

Whispered words at dawn,
The heat generated by a brush of flesh.
Electric shocks pulsing through my muscles after a lingering glance.
The wildfire raging in my stomach
Every time we're in the same room.
Heart pounding in my chest so violently rapid,
It is a stampede of wild horses
Threatening to burst through my rib cage.
Your distinct aroma wafting through my room
And lingering even after you're gone.
Wishing to see you if only to be near you.

Looking at you I know this is what love is:
That goofy smile painted on your face when she walks in the room
The exuberantly giddy rhythm of your voice when you say her name
Those probing eyes that linger on her until she makes eye contact
You falling on your face after attempting to do a backflip
Love is what you give her and what I secretly want with you.

I desire...

No heartache that rips my heart from my chest
Like how one of Zeus's lightning bolts tears through the sky
No tears that stream down my face like rain on a car windshield
No guilt weighing me down like an anchor holding down a ship.
I wish you loved me the way you love her.

Rebekah Schein
Onalaska, WI

'Twas the Night Before the Ides

'Twas the night before the Ides and all through the village
not a person was stirring, not even a sword.
Statues were decorated by the village square
in hopes that their great Caesar would soon be there.
Brutus and them all snuggled in beds,
while visions of stabbing danced in their heads.
And Cassius in his kerchief and Metellus in his cap
had just settled down for a long violent nap.
When, in the village, there rose such a clatter,
the villagers rose to see what's the matter.
Away to the window Antony flew like a flash,
tore open the shutters and threw up the sash.
The blood on the breast of the newly paved road
gave luster of midday to objects below.
When, to the villagers eyes did appear,
but a dead Caesar with thirty-five wounds.
With a jealous old man so sly and quick,
the villagers knew it must be Brutus.
More surprised than presents the villagers came
and called them by name:
Now Brutus! Now Cinna! Now Decius and Metellus!
On Casca! On Trebonius!
Oh! On pain and sorrow! To the devil you will go.
Now go away, go away all.

Samantha Renee Grembecki
Denver, NC

281

Love Is Hidden

Cold sand sifting through my fingers
Like my life through God's
How can something so simple
Be so incredibly odd?
Something that's pure
And something that's true
Abandons people daily
Just when it is due
Cruelty is found
In the oddest of places
Like a happy bunch of clowns
Making frightening faces
People can fly
To heights unknown
Like the smile on her face
When his is shown
Laughter is medicine
For those who are unwell
Like skin cream for people
Whose faces all swell
What this is trying to say
Is things that are gone
Are really just here
Represented by pawns

Cassandra Tagert
Richmond, VA

I Am

Your love has been kind over the years, and it
always lets me know where I stand, 'cause your heart
is pure when you stretch out your hand, and because
of you: *I am*

And things could have been so differently, if only
we had rejected each other and not given a damn,
but things didn't turn out that way, and because
of you: *I am*

I am because I have been set free, *I am* because
of your love for me, *I am* because of all that we
see, *I am* because I am free to *be*

And it is wonderful to be this way, so happy and
so carefree, and I thank my lucky stars until
this very day that I live in this reality

I am because I have been set free, *I am* because
of your love for me, *I am* because of all that
we see, *I am* because I am free to *be*

I am because I have been set free, *I am* because
of your love for me, *I am* because of all that we
see, *I am* because I am free to *be*

I am

Tadaram Alasadro Maradas
Alameda, CA

*Tadaram Maradas, whose real name is David Williams, is a writer and
author from the San Francisco Bay Area. He is alumni of Excelsior College
in Upstate New York, Villanova University in southeast Pennsylvania, and
the University of Maryland University College at Adelphi, Maryland. He
recently capped a satisfying twenty-four-year career in the United States
Army where he served in four contingency operations which included
both combative and non-combative operations. Since that time, poetry has
become his mainstay and his creativity is currently being highlighted through
his expression of poetry in lyric and rhyme. Tadaram Maradas is an active
member of the Academy of American Poets and a featured poet in the
International Who's Who in Poetry and the Best Poets and Poems of 2012.*

Sweet Poison

The bleakness of the moon setting
Is like a light smothered by the dark
And within the night she lies
In a maudlin heap
Beneath the teary night
Sucking on sin

It is not sweet nor bitter
But has a sting, an enticing sting,
As pleasant as candy

She sucks and sucks
Until the stings subdue
Watching the world
Tough yet sad
Putting on her mask
Emotionless yet harsh

The weight I am used to, she will say
The tears I overcame, she will think
The pain I forgot, she will lie

So tonight she lies
In a maudlin heap
Beneath the teary night
Sucking on sin

Jihyeon Joung
Houston, TX

Cattle Trucks and Train Rides

I'm put on a cattle truck outside of my house,
Tons of tall men, not one the size of a mouse.
They carry guns and helmets as they stand so still,
Awaiting us all to feel their cold chill.

The cattle truck leaves and reality hits me,
What kind of horrors lie in the path to see?
Do my brothers and sister wonder the same?
Maybe they're thinking this is just a game.

My father looks at me with tears in his eyes,
My mother cries as she says her goodbyes.
Why would she say these things, won't we still be together?
Maybe or maybe not, I don't know, I'm not that clever.

We arrive at the train station, so sad and so gloomy.
Then we are on the train which is not very roomy.
The train leaves and everyone starts to cry.
What is the matter, are we going to die?

Next thing I know, we've arrived at so-called Auschwitz.
The guards yell as they push and pull at everyone who comes off.
I'm led with other kids to a room that's so narrow and so dark.
A mist fills the room and I have trouble breathing,
I then see a bright light with an angel at the end.
Although this tragedy hurt my people, it didn't make us bend.

Logan Jarrod Sherrill
Sherrills Ford, NC

Growing up, I was always interested in reading, writing, and history. It seemed as if I would always have some historical fiction story to write down on a piece of paper. I wanted to make people laugh and cry as they read my stories; I wanted to fake a horrible event in history and bring some enlightenment out of the characters. However, now that I'm thirteen years old, I realize that when you're writing about tragic things, you shouldn't sugarcoat it. You need to tell the story and get it across to the audience, and that's what my target was when writing "Cattle Trucks and Train Rides."

Little Moments

Bright sun beats down this early afternoon.
Dry, yellowed grass lays flat like the back of an old horse.
Shiny black crow boys "echo-squawk" through
  the palest blue expanse of sky.
Young transulscent grape leaves gently sway
  in nature's slight breeze,
    seemingly straining to reach the Heavens.
Chorus of wind chimes sound their melodies.
Busy bees flit about from flower to flower. . .
    . .a.hello, then a goodbye. . .
A private plane soars above,
  mimicking those same little garden bees,
So goes the life of a retiree. . me!

Nancy West
Hayward, CA

The Blossom of Love

After the mighty winds, showers, and storms,
That is when love for another dies or transforms.
There are going to be times where it rains, sleets, and snows,
It is after those times, the blossom of love either dies or shows.
After the storm and the rains,
That is when love can make gains.
You and another will either make it through together,
Or your love will be broken and destroyed by the weather.
Your love for another may be damaged and need repair,
But you decide if you want to go on alone or as a pair.
True love is more than just loving words you declare,
It is being there for each other, even in times that tear.
There are going to be times where your love is put to the test
And times where it is going to be pushed, pulled, and stressed.
There will be times where you'll really have to invest
And deal with tough issues, that need to be addressed,
But if you can make your love last through the challenges that loom,
The most sensational flower will eventually open up and bloom.

Teresa Marie Binder
Marshfield, WI

Carl

The room is dark
A last-breath sound
Hearts plummet to ground
Heads bow, tears fall
Arms bid haste to comfort all

The room is light
Broken made whole
Rebirth of soul
Past loves call
Arms bid haste to welcome all

Print tells the tale
Words viewed with thought
Glimpse of a life caught
An interesting run
Wonder of all past done

Plans undone
Wished more time
No reason or rhyme
Alone I roam
I'm still visiting, but you're already home

Carol Ann Tamburo
Highgate Center, VT

Sabotage

Your words are the knives
which I use to whittle away
my imperfections, my
flaws—are they not beauty?
Monroe—so celebrated yet so
disrespected, yes, I am.

But I hope to one day
pluck away my unruly tangles
and reveal my inner glowing self,
glowing like the desert:
vast, smooth, yet
empty.
Is this innocence?
My once young self,
so smooth and pure
to the inner demons which now
plague my haunted mind,
choke my voice
until I am silenced in a world
in which I am nothing,
trapped by expectation,
deemed unworthy by
reality—oh, so cruel and unrelenting
yet the truth. . .

Matthew Dwelle
Fairfield, CT

Need

winter seeds' diapason
soaring at night
in temperance of trees
to superscription
in reliquary of lights
with its baton
advancing syntax
of forever rising glee
in bread
of the angels' town
releases view
of mansions and raptors
in shining shadows
looming loud
in their length
silent and still,
finally the raptor
with lens perfection
in surveyor's eye
sets the point
and talons thrive
off on wing
in argosy of glory,
and long the mansion
remains insouciant
still and smug

Michael Kirby Smith
Baltimore, MD

Society

I have not a reason to live anymore,
Heartbeats are limited, veins so sore.
With every breath I gasp for, each inhale I take,
I realize not giving up sooner was my only mistake.
By the time you read this I will be dead and gone,
My body will be lifeless when you awake at dawn.
No need to mourn as I know you don't really care,
Save the tears, in my life you were never there.
As you stand over and stare at my cold, draining body,
Remember that I won't be missed, and for this blessing,
You can thank society. . .

Austin Texas Houston Kelley
Carlisle, PA

Rapture

We watch Apollo paint the horizon and disappear into the water
while walking hand in hand on a remote, pristine beach.
Civilization is a faint light in the distance—just out of reach.

Strolling sky clad—our bodies are being caressed
and invigorated by Neptune's cool sea breeze.
As the moon goddess illuminates the dusk
and ascends to her throne in the heavens—
we are captivated by the moonlight in each other's eyes
and are instantly drawn together like magnets.
Lost in a gaze, we become intertwined like beach wood
and drop to our knees.

Time is of no concern—for we are in a realm of the gods—
where years are like days.
Being fueled by the spirits of fire
our yearning ignites into a blaze.

Overcome with passion—
like ocean to beach—we experience wave after wave of pleasure.
Embraced by each other—we lie on the warm, silky white sand—
enjoying the cosmos and thinking this is a gift from the gods
that we will always treasure.

Deborah Leah Kelley
Alachua, FL

The Best Change

can you hear my wild wolf cries.
can you see my riverly tears flow from my eyes.
can you feel my heartbeat start to race,
at a fast pace like a race car in a Daytona 500 race
the way i fall, the way i crawl.
reaching out for help with no one around
i slowly start to drown. the pain from it all
drove me insane for years, but now
there's nothing but happy cheers from the way
i recovered now hover with lots of love.
flying free like a dove.
i'm stepping in the right direction.
rising up in my own resurrection.
changing my ways to have better days.
sun rays brighter days with the help of god
and his angels i pray too.
i have pulled on though my life's roller coaster.
i had my ups and my downs.
my smiles and my frowns.
now i wear my calmness crown.

Heather Marie Bleakley
Wappingers Alls, NY

*I am a twenty-one-year-old girl with Asperger's. I wrote this poem about how I
suffer with mood and behavior problems. I've had numerous hospitalizations
and I've been out for a year now, the longest I've ever been doing well. It's
like a whole new me. I wrote about my life experiences. I recently lost my
grandma. She is the one who inspired me to write poetry, so I dedicate this
poem to my grandma. This one is for you, Grandma.*

Index of Poets

CPSIA information can be obtained at www.ICGtesting.com
Printed in the USA
BVOW03s0017210314

348309BV00001B/60/P